Ice and Fire

Thawing a Murderer's Heart

Baldur Einarsson

Copyright © Baldur Einarsson 2024

All Rights Reserved

No part of this publication may be reproduced, distributed, or transmitted in any form or by any means, including photocopying, recording, or other electronic or mechanical methods, without the author's prior written permission, except in the case of brief quotations embodied in critical reviews and certain other non-commercial uses permitted by copyright law. For permission requests, please get in touch with the author.

Contents

Endorsements i
Dedication vii
Acknowledgements ix
Foreword xi
About the Author xiv
Epilogue 1
1 THE ASSAULT 2
2 FATHER FIGURES 13
3 THE CARETAKER 24
4 SECRET LIVES 31
5 THE KING! 37
6 MY COUSIN AARON 44
7 THE DEATH OF LOVE 51
8 HIGH SCHOOLING 59
9 STARING AT COFFINS 63
10 A LIGHTBULB MOMENT 72
11 CROSSING THE LINE 83
12 THE DEBT COLLECTOR 90
13 CLASHING WITH COPS 100
14 THE CRACKS APPEAR 106
15 VENGEANCE IS MINE 117
16 THE GREEN-EYED MONSTER 122
17 YOU HAVE BEEN WARNED 126
18 JUDGMENT DAY 136
19 INSIDE 143
20 GRADUATION DAY 150
21 HALFWAY HOUSE 155
22 ON MY KNEES 165
23 SIMPLY THE BEST 174
24 TEARING DOWN THE WALLS 182
25 PUNCHING OR PRAYING 186
26 BE NOT AFRAID 191
27 THE RESTORATION 198
28 A HUG FROM DAD 203
29 GOLD 211
30 TO FORGIVE 217
31 A SON IS BORN 222
32 HEY, LITTLE SISTER 226
33 BLESS THIS HOUSE! 235
34 I CHOOSE HIM! 242
35 OUR LITTLE MIRACLE 249
36 SOPHIE'S LEGACY 253
37 FEARLESS LOVE 263
38 DON'T GIVE UP! 268

Endorsements

Baldur Einarsson's story is not for the faint of heart. Your heart will be torn in two as you read of the injustice he endured, the injustice he witnessed, and the injustice he committed. The power of the love of God will bring you to tears as Baldur shares how Abba Father melted his heart and brought healing and redemption into his life. Testimonies like his declare the undeniable power of the cross of Christ to transform lives. Thank you, Baldur, for sharing with such deep vulnerability and transparency. You are defeating the enemy through the blood of the Lamb and the bold word of your witness. (Rev 12:11)

John Arnott
Founder, Catch the Fire

Biographies are inspirational. They give us a behind-the-scenes look into the life of the author. What they did right, what they did wrong, how they responded to tragedy, etc. This book is raw because Baldur's story is raw. The abuse that he has suffered and the circumstances that came Baldur's way had some very tragic consequences. But, and this is a big but, Baldur had an encounter that massively changed the trajectory of his life from crime, prostitution, and drugs into one of the most dramatic lifestyle changes anyone could hope for. This book tells you about that encounter and who the person is who changed Baldur's life.

Steve Long
Author of The Faith Zone, On the Run, My Healing Belongs to Me
Ambassador, Catch The Fire Toronto

Ice and Fire is not a book for the faint of heart. It is a raw and honest account of a man who suffered unimaginable pain and trauma but also experienced the healing power of God's grace and love. This book will challenge you, inspire you, and move you to tears. It is a testimony of how Jesus can transform even the most broken lives into beautiful stories of redemption. If you are looking for a book that will stir your soul and ignite your faith, Fire and Ice is the one for you.

Alyn Jones, co-pastor Goodly, Nashville, TN

Baldur Einarsson is nothing short of a miracle. With an extremely traumatic childhood, which led him to an inevitably dark place, it's incredible that he even survived, let alone thrived. Baldur is victorious.

He lives a vibrant and joyful life, has a beautiful wife and family, loves his job, and has a fruitful ministry. Baldur's experience hands a lifeline to those on the edge of hell because he himself knows exactly what it's like to be there.

Ice & Fire - Thawing of a murderer's heart is his riveting and touchingly beautiful story. Be prepared to laugh, weep, stay up late reading, and most of all, be astounded at how the power of Jesus' love can revolutionize a man and make him a voice of hope for so many.

Patricia Bootsma
Catch the Fire USA Co-National Outreach Director, Co-Pastor Catch the Fire Kansas City, Author of Raising Burning Hearts and The Desire of Jesus

I'm convinced that my friend, Pastor Baldur Einarsson, possesses unparalleled writing skills in Iceland. Immersing myself in his book has been a true delight, and I wholeheartedly encourage everyone to explore its pages. It has the potential to be a life-changing experience, fostering a stronger faith in Jesus Christ. Baldur's poignant account of his challenging childhood and upbringing in a difficult environment has the power to reshape one's perspective. Rather than succumbing to adversity, he emerged as a resilient and devout man. I take immense pride in calling Pastor Baldur my friend. Thank you, Pastor Baldur, for sharing your story through this impactful book.

Adnan Maqsood
Founder, director and CEO of Vision Tv

Employing over 1,000 employees and serving thousands of customers a day brings new situations and stories every day.

No matter each individual or the unique situation, there almost always involves emotional components such as shame, anger, hurt, rejection, etc. Navigating issues of the heart is first personal before it can be done effectively with others.

Baldur's journey of his own heart and experiences lead to encounters of God's truth in love touching each place so deeply and powerfully. While I encourage everyone to read this book for themselves, it will also only increase your capabilities as a leader of others, no matter the sphere of influence you may have.

David Anderson
(Franchisee for McDonald's, Owner of Pure Mosaic Records and minority owner in the soccer club NCFC)

I have enjoyed the good fortune of reviewing and working on some pretty powerful stories, including the Queen of Katwe. But this one, well, this one is different. It pulls, pushes, tugs, scratches, claws and cuts, but in the end, much like a rugged cross-fit workout, you feel better having endured the exercise.

Baldur and his story are both raw and transparent. You will love him, you will despise him, you will envy him and you will pity him but he and his story will inevitably and inherently challenge you to become the best version of who you are truly meant to be".

Troy A. Buder
TABu Filmz - Founder/President
Producer - Queen of Katwe (Disney)

I am absolutely thrilled to endorse my friend, Baldur Einarsson's incredible book, Ice and Fire. From the word go, I was completely engaged and captivated by the story's gripping storyline, raw emotion, and the complex characters brought to life on its pages.

Baldur's writing is so vivid, masterful, and descriptive that I felt like I was living in the moment and experiencing every twist and turn with him - which was truly moving.

Baldur invites you to explore the depths of the human heart and, more than anything, the enduring magical power of the human spirit. For me, this was not just a book; it was an experience that stayed with me long after I turned the final page.

Congratulations on a fantastic book, Baldur!

Sincerely,
Surprise S. Sithole
The Author of Voice in the Night

I found Baldur's story quite captivating. His telling of it takes you on quite a ride - from a life that began in the depths of heartbreaking darkness, eventually to the freedom that only comes from personally encountering the reality of the living God and the transformation that comes with being 'born of the Spirit'..... I believe the reader will find themselves inspired to embrace all that God has provided for us."

William J. Fowler
Retired Multiple Business Owner
Current Consultant to Business Exec's and Mentees

An incredible story of overcoming and total surrender to God. In an impactful way, Baldur openly and transparently shares the darkest moments of his life and how God, in His infinite mercy, not only rescues him—who previously was not showing life—but transforms him into a generator of life. In each chapter, you will be sure that it doesn't matter how or where you are, but God is looking at you and calling you closer. You will be moved and impacted by this incredible life story.

Anderson Lima

From the starting sentences of Baldur's first chapter you are immediately gripped and immersed into his story as if it is happening in real time. His words both honest and articulate, do not leave a detail to be missed. In his book, Fire and Ice, you see Baldur's soul laid open and bare and when it feels like the night can't get any darker... the incredible, merciful, and graciously kind hand of God comes and pulls us all in to an embrace of light. Baldur earnestly shares the courage and faith it takes to continuously humble ourselves before God and surrender to Him. This book shows both the depths of despair, evil, and suffering of the world and yet the deeply forgiving, purifying love of God who can not only make sense of it all but redeems it all. When man may seem utterly lost to the world, the true author and finisher of our story says, "Yet I, God.

Rev. Dr. Susanne Baldeosingh

Dedication

To my wife - the beacon of my heart. Thank you.

To our children, whose contagious laughter fills our home with joy.

To my extended family and cherished friends, both near and far, whose unwavering support and love have been my stronghold through my journey toward healing.

To the compassionate souls in our international community, your solidarity has been a source of immense strength and inspiration.

To Troy Buder, whose encouragement contributed significantly to my perseverance. Your support has been an invaluable part of this experience, helping me navigate challenges with a much steadier hand. Thank you.

I also extend my deepest gratitude to everyone involved in the creation and completion of this book. From the early drafts to the final touches, your expertise, insights, and dedication have been inestimable. To the editors, designers, and all the unseen hands that have shaped this work, your talent and commitment have turned a dream into a reality.

In crafting my story, all names except mine and my dear wife's have been altered with respect. This is my testament to the power of faith, the strength of community, and the unbreakable bonds of love that span time and continents. May it light your way as you have illuminated mine. To all who stand at a crossroads, believing every door has closed: please remember - no path is truly impassable, and the way home is always within reach.

With genuine gratitude, deep appreciation, and a hopeful spirit, this dedication opens the book.

Acknowledgments

First and foremost, I extend my deepest gratitude to my wife, whose unwavering support was my anchor while navigating the turbulent process of writing this story. Her love and assistance were crucial in shaping the narrative, and her patience in my moments of doubt was a beacon of hope.

I am profoundly thankful to my children, whose faith in me was both humbling and inspiring. Your belief in my vision and your awe-inspiring spirits have enriched this journey immeasurably.

A special thank you goes to Troy Buder, whose enthusiastic encouragement and meticulous attention to detail pushed us to refine the manuscript relentlessly, striving for near perfection.

To my mother and brothers, thank you for your unwavering support and solidarity as I navigated this deeply personal venture. Your backing during such a vulnerable period of self-expression was indispensable to my perseverance and confidence.

Emma, your final touches transformed the manuscript. The text has been through many tests, and your amazing contributions made all the difference in bringing it to its final form. Thank you for your critical eye and perfectionist touch.

To all those who have been a part of this journey—friends, colleagues, and mentors—you know who you are. Your collective wisdom and encouragement have been invaluable. I am eternally grateful for every conversation, every word of encouragement, and every moment of support.

Foreword

We were on an open trolly under the Dominican Republic sky, with leaders from all over the world, when I first met Baldur. The only thing I knew about him was that he was from Iceland, had blonde Viking-like hair, and his eyes had a tint of clear sea blue that suggested he'd lived an easy, peaceful life. The type with a healthy, stable family, who charmed all the girls in high school and was the star soccer player. I couldn't have been more wrong.

This man had suffered so many hurts. Hurts trampled under disappointments and even more hurt. Baldur was a living, breathing example of the effects of an abusive upbringing on a child. From suffering cruelty from coming and going stepfathers to caring for an alcoholic mother and facing betrayal from almost everyone who should have loved and looked out for him. For young Baldur, life was one long, silent scream in a dark sea of drugs, violence, prison, depression, and hate.

I once saw a snake lying on a road, twisting in pain after a car had run it over. Baldur's heart was that snake. Beginning with a 7-year-old boy curled up in a fetal position on a cold kitchen floor. I still wonder how so much hurt and horror can be crammed into one little boy. How can one little person twist and writhe in so much pain and still go on? Still, breathe?

Living on the run from the police, peers and other frightening criminals, Baldur was ferociously chased by the indescribable guilt and rage that gnawed at him like a ravenous sick rat. But he kept on.

He fought on. Punching… and getting punched. Now, as a man, he writes with short punches to the head and often straight to the heart.

I once read that we were all born on fire, full of wild desires, and what we do with this fire is our spirituality. What this fire did in Baldur is a spiritual odyssey. I have read many criminals to God books, and I thank God for each and everyone, but this story is different. Reading this book was like sitting with Baldur in the kitchen, with his elbows on the table and the blood still on his hands. You may feel unsafe at times, you may feel distaste and confusion, but you'll want to listen to this man all night because you will feel how much of what is in him is in you. Your wounds, your fears. We are also not safe from Baldur's God, who shows up halfway through his story. This God breaks into Baldur's world in wonderful, crazy, painful, and sometimes very funny ways. After a miracle and healing, there is a punch in the gut and a loss, and the spark of fire in his heart seems to fall again into the ice, but somehow, Baldur always rises again. Not just as a spark but as a bonfire. In my minds-eye, I can see an insane asylum in hell, full of demons who tried their best to discourage Baldur. "We just couldn´t get that guy!" they moan, over and over again, in strait jackets.

One afternoon, In the bathroom of a hospital, where his girlfriend lay bleeding, Baldur snorted some crack, then looked up at himself in the mirror - "Look at you, taking it up the nose in a public toilet while your girlfriend is lying there after losing your baby."

Then, he took another hit anyway. The Bible is called a mirror, too, because it is filled with stories of people who have the same courage to really look at themselves.

This is not a typical Christian book where everything is bad before Christ and everything is good after. The furious fire of God had to burn deep into this man's heart.

How does a man come to Christ, attend church, devour the Bible, and still run a whorehouse? Baldur's "normal" was off the charts, but the fire of God often burns through the coldest ice, and that brothel was transformed into a church, with Baldur as the pastor.

Baldur and his wife Barbara spearheaded 'Stay Alive', a program designed to free Iceland from the cruelty of addiction and its consequences. Their passion and fire are conquering the black ice, and just like the day a young Baldur heard God whisper to him, "Stand up, Baldur. I love you," today may be such a day for you. Stand up. He loves you.

Today, as co-owners of the Lausnin Family and Trauma Centre, Baldur and his wife restore many families, couples, and individuals. How will it end, though?

Perhaps, as Robert Frost wrote, "in fire." The fire of wild love.

Pastor Andrew McMillan
Medellin, Colombia

About the Author

Baldur's story is one of resilience and profound transformation, reflecting the strength of the human spirit. He emerged from a troubled childhood marked by abuse, spiraling into violence and eventually leading to incarceration for serious crimes. Despite this, Baldur found a turning point, embracing a new path of spirituality and education. Now, he leads Iceland's one of the top Family and Trauma Center, guiding others out of darkness and offering hope and inspiration to those seeking redemption.

Baldur's book, Ice and Fire, is a passion project through which he has poured his creative heart out. He eagerly anticipates hearing the opinions of his readers, knowing that his story has the potential to resonate deeply with those who have faced similar struggles. Through his writing, Baldur aims to ignite a spark of hope and courage in others, encouraging them to embrace their own journeys of healing and transformation.

Get in touch with Baldur:

Epilogue

In the quiet moments of reflection that bring this book to a close, I extend my gratitude to you, dear reader. Your journey through these pages is a gift not only of your time but of your spirit.

I must give my thanks to God, my soul's compass, who gives me the courage to look at myself honestly and the fortitude to deal with life's challenges. It was through life's toughest and most harrowing times that I've felt God's most profound love and mercy the most, guiding me toward hope and renewal.

I'm here as a testament to the possibility of rebirth. Proof that we can change and grow, especially when we have supportive, loving people around us. Life is never a solitary endeavor. We are all notes in one grand composition woven by the hand of God. A society that harmonizes in support of those who have stumbled and extends a hand that lifts them back into the melody of the whole.

Let's aim for a world where we learn from our struggles, grow wiser through our collective tribulations, and steer the lost away from the shadows and into the light.

As long as the breath of life flows through us, the flames of hope dance unextinguished!

So, with a heart full of thanks, hope and faith, I say: Thank you, and may God's boundless love guide you on your journey ahead.

Part One

1

THE ASSAULT

I was seven years old when it happened. Seven years old and at home with my mother and two younger siblings. Out of nowhere, a fierce fist suddenly pounded threateningly on the front door, and that sinking, all too familiar fear radiated through our little apartment. Mom stood wide-eyed and frozen in terror, holding onto Sophie (3) and David (2), her unpacked suitcases still at her feet.

Furious fists pounded vehemently on the door again. Then we heard the voice that they belonged to.

Violent. Insistent. Enraged.

We didn't need anyone to tell us who it was.

More manic, savage pounding and shouting, then...

Thud! The front door flew open, slamming deafeningly against the wall. He stood there, breathless and staring... hatred in his wild, frenzied eyes.

Rikki. My mom's boyfriend. My stepfather.

Ice and Fire

I looked anxiously across from him to Mom, terror coursing through my little body like an icy current. Mom's face was frozen and pale, pleading over the piercing, petrified shrieks of the toddlers, now holding onto her legs for dear life. Rikki's eyes settled on me first, as they often did, burning with animosity. Then, without even so much as a blink, he lifted the sobbing, terrified Sophie and David, the children he had fathered, and carried them into their bedroom. We stood in stunned silence as he tucked them carefully into their beds and turned on a soothing melody on a cassette player before quietly closing the door and turning the key in the lock.

I watched him in breathless suspense, feeling sick, knowing that absolutely nothing good could ever come from him in this state.

Mom moved closer to me. I desperately wanted to be a huge rock that she could hide behind, but I was just one little boy caught in the crossfire.

"Now…who did you go to Amsterdam with, you bitch?" he spat out menacingly, lunging at us both and gripping aggressively at Mom's shoulder. I watched on, horrified, at his face up against hers, offloading a barrage of offensive insults and disgusting profanities, when Mom let out a harrowing, guttural cry.

A primal, impetuous rage suddenly surged within me.

Enough!

Filled with an unexpected wave of courage, I ran at Rikki and leaped onto his back, desperate to free my mother from his raging grasp. I held on with all the strength I could muster, but he just shook me off like a feather and hurled me, tumbling onto the floor. Useless.

When I looked up, my stepfather was beating my mother to a pulp.

Her blood sprayed across her face from his pulverizing blows. His brutal, thick, bloodied fists rained down on her relentlessly as she cried out,

"Rikki! Babe! Please...please don't do this!" She pleaded. He kept going.

His remorseless, frenzied punches continued until Mom managed to dodge a blow, ending with his fist punching straight through a window to the sound of shattering glass. A puddle of blood formed, dripping at Rikki's feet as he growled, seething through clenched teeth,

"Look what you've done, you stupid bitch!"

Battered and bloodied, Mom struggled to her feet and desperately fumbled in a kitchen drawer for a dishcloth to hand to him. "Rikki, honey, you're right...ok... but please wrap this around your hand to stop the bleeding."

I watched him as he slowly and deliberately wrapped the cloth around his wrist, praying it was all over. The silence was deafening as he took a deep breath and glared across at Mom again, utter contempt in his eyes. Then came the accusations and insults again as he stalked threateningly, red-faced, towards her.

Then- SMACK!

Blood gushed from my mom's nose as she crumpled onto the floor, motionless, reeling from the impact.

SMACK! SMACK!

He wasn't done.

Rikki glared down at her, triumphant and smirking, as I sat in the corner, rigid and trembling with terror. Was my mom dead?

Then, out of the corner of my eye, I saw something gleaming. It was the big knife from the kitchen drawer…in Rikki's hand. He turned to me smugly and shouted, "Watch boy!" as he knelt, breathing heavily over my mom's unconscious body, stroking her hair. He unfastened the top of her blouse and shouted again, "Look at me, you little Bastard! Look at me!"

I looked.

He pressed the tip of the knife to my mother's throat and, with a savage, sadistic laugh, taunted.

"Should I cut off your mama's head?"

I was speechless. Paralyzed. Powerless. "Brenda!"

A distressed, insistent voice suddenly pierced the thick air. "Brenda!! What's going on in there?!"

I watched on, shaking and numb, as two large and imposing police officers suddenly burst into our apartment towards Rikki. The knife fell to the floor…and when I looked up from it again, he was gone.

Handcuffed and led to the police car waiting outside.

My terror turned to relief as I ran over to hold my mom. But it wasn't over. This was not the first time; I knew it wouldn't be the last…and just like the last time, the cops encouraged Mom to take refuge at the women's shelter. Our shattered little family from Keflavik, Iceland, is on the move again. Physically removed from our abuser, but still absolutely chained to him, emotionally.

A short while after that, my crushed, dispirited mom was sent to rehab, and I was left alone, confused, and terrified that she would never come home. I was sent out to the East of Iceland to my grandparents (Rikki's parents). They were kind people, always willing to help and care for me despite their wicked, abusive son. When my nightmares woke me, shaking at night, my grandmother would be there, holding me gently as I lay curled up in a fetal position on the floor.

"This will never happen to you again, Baldur," she would promise. "Never…"

From that day on, whenever threatening situations arose, I always sought solace behind locked doors and in enclosed spaces, a kitchen knife in hand… just in case my vile stepfather came back. I was still afraid. Very afraid. A traumatized seven-year-old boy who had witnessed far too much in his short lifetime. Looking back, it wasn't the knife or his blows that hurt me the most; his words cut far more deeply than any knife ever could. They made me feel worthless, helpless, and completely insignificant. I could only imagine the impact they had on Mom.

After every assault, in his usual malicious style, Rikki would wickedly add insult to injury. He would walk smugly into the kitchen, look at my mom and smirk, clearly revolted by her black eyes, cuts, and split lips.

"Brenda, come on! You look disgusting!" he would sneer. "For God's sake, put on some makeup or sunglasses, woman!"

Then he'd laugh. Really funny…

So young, I'd watched these interactions, taking them in as normality but not really understanding what was happening. Over time, I even began to believe the filthy lies Rikki breathed and started to question my own mom's innocence. Maybe she had done something very wrong.

Maybe she deserved the beatings. Maybe Mom was bad. Maybe I was, too.

This is where it all began. My shame. This deep-down sense of being useless and unworthy of love. I was the microscopically tiny boy with a big knot in my stomach, who nobody wanted, and I was petrified of the unpredictability of the one person who was supposed to be my protector. My role-model. I never, ever felt safe with him.

One day, two years previously, when I was 5, Rikki, clearly in a good mood, offered to take me to the local swimming pool. He didn't have to ask twice! I jumped up and down and practically burst with excitement! Maybe he did like me after all! Hanging on to the hope of acceptance and maybe even a friendship with Rikki, I undressed in the changing room and ran to take a shower with him, chatting nonstop with excitement. I pulled on my favorite blue-and-red Speedos and galloped outside to the hot tub, jumping in with a huge splash. I grinned happily as the soothing water warmed my body.

Then, I felt Rikki watching me.

"Come here, kid," he said. "I want to show you something."

Ice and Fire

I lifted myself out of the hot tub and trotted along behind him happily, following with quick little wet steps to the deep end of the pool. "Come here!" he beckoned me. I tip-toed tentatively toward him, beginning to feel a little uneasy. His voice seemed suddenly cold.

Clinical. I looked up into his face, and there it was again…that smirk.

Before I knew it, he bent down, grabbed me around the waist, hoisted me up high, and tossed me flying into the deep end of the pool.

Panic overcame me as I hit the water with a smack and immediately started to sink. I gasped desperately for breath and thrashed about in fear as the water filled my mouth and nose. Somehow, after a moment, I managed to claw my way to the surface, only to hear the sound of Rikki's harsh, berating voice.

"Swim, you little bastard!" he shouted.

Panicking, I paddled and thrashed around like mad to avoid sinking again. I tried to see how far I was from the edge of the pool, but I couldn't figure out which direction to swim in. I saw Rikki standing at the pool's edge, laughing like a maniac, while I flailed about, drowning, for what seemed like a lifetime. As I struggled, coughing, I discovered that if I kicked my legs in a certain way, I could push myself toward the edge of the pool.

"You swim like a dog!" Rikki shouted at me. "Do you only know doggy- paddle?"

His manic laughter echoed in my ears as I finally managed to grab onto the side. My legs were sapped of strength, my heart was pounding, my lungs were burning… but only one thought raced through my mind.

I did it!

"Well, now you know how to swim!" Rikki spat. I did.

My stepfather's "sense of humor" was always a mystery to me. Simply put…he was a big bully. He bullied me. He bullied Mom. He even bullied his friends. Rikki used to work on fishing boats with a short, stocky man called Fredrick. Fredrick was kind and fun, and we would sometimes arm-wrestle each other. One time, when I lost, he said, "You'll grow big and strong if you eat your vegetables… especially onions!" I rushed excitedly into the kitchen, grabbed a giant onion from the fridge, and bit into it as if it were an apple. As soon as I finished the last burning morsel, I ran back out into the living room, tongue out, and challenged Fredrick to another round. Lo and behold, I beat him! The onion had given me the same super-human strength that spinach gave Popeye!

Victory!

Ice and Fire

Being my stepfather's best friend, you'd think that Fredrick would be exempt from his off-color bullying. But he wasn't. One Sunday, Mom, Rikki, Fredrick, and I were standing on the pier. The tide was out, the boats lay low by the dock, and the late Spring sun was about to set.

Happy with the day's haul and having moored their little fishing boat, Rikki suddenly grabbed Fredrick without warning and hurled him off the pier…straight into the freezing cold sea. Fredrick landed in the water with a loud splash several meters below, and we could hear his cries in the ice-cold water as he made his way towards the ladder leading back up to the pier.

Rikki just stood there on the wharf, laughing his head off, as poor Fredrick clambered up the freezing, seaweed-covered ladder, his soaking wet clothes hanging heavily from him. You see, no one was spared.

But now, at seven years old, the day of the traumatic assault in the apartment had changed me. My real feelings were now clear to me…

I hated Rikki, and I hated all the Rikki's of the world. I suddenly felt an intense sense of purpose - I would no longer be weak and powerless. I would be strong! I would be in control! I would crush all the bullies!

Baldur Einarsson

Being such a young witness to a woman's submissiveness to a man's merciless cruelty, the day Rikki beat my mother to a pulp, I made a vow.

"When I grow up - nobody will ever hurt or humiliate me or my mom ever again."

Excerpt from Child Protective Services report no. 24, December 11, 1988

The interview takes a more serious turn.

It is noted that Baldur calls his stepfather 'Dad,' stating he's afraid to call him anything else, as he may hurt him like he had when he was little. Baldur stated that his stepfather frequently hurt him in his sleep, but he never said anything.

Baldur says his stepfather also spanks his sister, Sophie. He illustrates this by striking the desk in front of him forcefully. He also mentions several additional incidents of Rikki's violent tendencies. It is clear that Baldur doesn't understand his stepfather and fears for his life.

Although Baldur provides the above information freely and without hesitation, he is extremely anxious that this information might make its way back to the stepfather. I have promised him all possible confidentiality in this regard.

2
FATHER FIGURES

Our family moved house a lot while Mom and Rikki were together. Thirteen times, to be precise, I later found out. I was too young to have a clear sense of how long we stayed in each place, but it was very disorienting for me, and I had no idea why we had to keep moving.

Looking back now, I realize we were basically on the run. At least Rikki was. Maybe we were constantly uprooted because the ongoing sounds of domestic violence prompted neighbors from all thirteen towns to call in complaints? I'll never know.

I do know, however, according to reports, that after a year of living in the Westman Islands, we moved back to the small town of Keflavik. Of the few clear memories that I do have of this time, I remember that I was finally allowed to own a pet. I was over the moon! We got a beautiful cat, and we named him Bowie. I absolutely adored my new companion.

Playing outside with him, one day, as I always did, I was suddenly approached by the woman who lived next door to us. She was clearly furious and shouted angrily at me, pointing her finger at Bowie -

"That cat of yours got into my house again! If he so much as steps foot in there one more time, I'll cut his head off! And that's a promise!"

I watched her storm off, enraged, as tears streamed down my cheeks. I ran inside to my mother, holding Bowie, horrified and crying.

"What happened, honey?" my mom asked.

"The neighbor is going to kill our kitty!" I wailed. "She said she's going to cut Bowie's head off if he comes into her house one more time!"

"That's it!" She marched off into the sitting room, "Enough is enough!" she shouted as I followed her, still crying.

"Rikki, you need to go and talk to that terrible woman. Honestly - threatening to kill a child's pet is taking things way too far!"

I watched Rikki nervously from behind Mum. He listened, sitting back in his chair, cool as a cucumber, paused, then stood up and began to hum - almost joyfully. He put on his trousers and a t-shirt, and I followed cautiously behind him as he walked down the hall and put on his shoes, still humming. He then opened the front door, but instead of walking up the footpath to the neighbor's house, he ran suddenly towards the fence that separated our two gardens, and though the fence looked a lot taller than Rikki, he cleared it in one go.

I could still hear him humming.

I was very nervous as he pounded on the neighbor's door. She often scolded and intimidated me when I was playing outside, so I had no idea what was going to happen next. As soon as she opened the door, Rikki's casual humming turned into a frightening, dissonant roar! "How dare you… you stupid hag! How dare you threaten to kill our cat!"

Of course, Rikki didn't stop there either. He did what he did best and wove together a litany of ear-piercing threats; swear words and insults that rained down upon the neighbor. Watching, gobsmacked, from our side of the fence, I nudged my mom and whispered,

"You can't hear her at all!"

"No," mom whispered back, smiling slightly. "She's totally tongue-tied."

I watched Rikki with sudden admiration as he turned back around, cleared the fence again and walked toward us, "She's definitely never coming anywhere near your cat again," he whispered to me conspiratorially as he stroked my cheek. He walked past me and sat back down in his TV chair as if nothing had happened.

My heart swelled! He had done for me what real dads do for their boys. He'd actually taken my side!

The very next day, the neighbor approached me again, but this time, she smiled and handed me a small bag. The bag was filled with all kinds of miniature packets of exciting brands of breakfast cereal and candy I'd never seen before. She must have bought them at the American military base, which was in our little town at the time. I felt victorious and proud because Rikki had finally acted like my father. He'd set an example and taught me how to get strangers to bend to my will.

But, a good example, and my father, he was not.

For as long as he and my mother were together, I believed that Rikki was my father. I was even named after him: Baldur Freyr Rikharðsson. Only, finally, once they were divorced, did my mom tell me the whole truth. My father was someone else entirely.

My real father's name was Einar, and I was told that if I wanted to, I could finally meet him. This new information threw me totally off guard and, of course, raised a whole new slew of difficult, existential questions in my little mind: Why didn't I know about him? Why hadn't he come to my rescue before now? And, last but not least, why had he not wanted to be my dad until now? Only when I was much older did my mother eventually shed light on these painful issues. My father had, in fact, tried to keep in touch with me at first, but there were consequences, as you can imagine, if Rikki found out. So…my dad had stopped calling.

Upon reflection, I could understand my father's decision. But wasn't I worth it? I answered myself and believed my own lie so thoroughly that I became utterly convinced of my own worthlessness.

Rikki, however, was just one of the many men who entered and exited my world, hooking up with my mom and then playing the part of the man of the house to our little broken family.

Men like Halli, my mom's next boyfriend and my next role model. After Rikki left, Halli swaggered into our world and filled it with fun, color, and chaos! He was in an Icelandic rock band called "Rimlarokk," which was made up of ex-cons who had recorded an album while all its members were in prison. Halli was just really, really cool. He showed me how to slick my hair back with gel, taught me how to tie a bandana around my head and introduced me to Icelandic rock legend Bubbi Morthens. Halli, in his time with us, also taught me all there was to know about drugs, stimulants, and how to get away with crime. My young, impressionable mind excitedly soaked up everything he had to say. He told me crazy, animated stories about prison life, fighting, and what it was really like doing time. He knew it all, and man, I idolized him!

One afternoon, while we were chatting, I asked him, worried, "Why is Mom always lying half asleep on the sofa in the daytime?"

"It's ok, kid, your mom's just shot herself up with morphine," he replied. "It's good for her. When she feels bad, she needs to be able to just lie there and sleep it off."

It was good for her. She was just resting. So, I just hung out with him instead. He was fun to be around and never mean to me. He showed me how to do push-ups and flex my barely-there little muscles. I wasn't afraid of anything as long as Halli was with us. "Don't be scared of old Rikki," he'd joke. "If he comes anywhere near you, I'll pulverize him and shove cocaine up his ass! I'll really make it sting!"

He was brilliant, and I saw my future when I looked at Halli. I could just picture it all: I'd sell dope, beat up anyone who got in my way, and play guitar and sing at parties. I finally had a friend and father figure I could respect.

But that didn't last. One day, without any warning or explanation, Halli simply disappeared from our lives. I was left behind with the song he taught me, a bandana, and a deep longing to live Halli's kind of life. The cool life. I wanted to be grown up and strong, be a party animal who drank and smoked. I resolved to be a bad boy like him. It was my new normal to have people appearing and disappearing from my life, but he was kinder to me than Rikki ever was.

Having been left with this example of how to be a real man, I began to find joy in being a bit mischievous. I'd find half-smoked cigarettes outside on the street, light them up and pretend to smoke like a man. Never inhaling but feeling so grown up and tough just holding a cigarette between my fingers. I also decided to give drinking a go. Wanting to see what it was all about, I'd sneak into the kitchen, grab a chair and reach far up for Mom's vodka bottles inside the kitchen cabinet. I'd quickly take a hefty swig and almost spit it out as it burnt my mouth so badly. It tasted revolting! Ugh! Why was mom always drinking this awful stuff?

But I wanted to grow up and grow up fast, so I always took another swig before quietly replacing the bottle and climbing down as if it had never happened.

During this period, you could say I started to become a bit of a handful. One day, when I was home alone, I grabbed a big knife from the kitchen, stripped down to my underwear, stuck the knife in the elastic waistband and started swinging on the bunk bed in our room. I was Tarzan- in the mist, muscular, swinging between the trees in the jungle. I was a courageous hero, defeating all the evil in our one-bedroom apartment. I pounded at my chest, let out Tarzan's trademark cry: "Ooooooooo- ooohhh-ooooooh!" gripped the bunk bed frame and swung back and forth dramatically before landing with a crash on my mother's bed... and the massive kitchen knife lodged deep into my thigh! With blood gushing from my leg, I grabbed onto the knife and jiggled it back and forth, but it wasn't going anywhere. I didn't want to go to the hospital- I would get into trouble, and they'd probably give me a shot! Mom's first aid kit! The little green box that always fixed everything. I felt a strange pressure as if something was trying to burst out of my leg, so trying not to cry, I tore off a length of gauze, placed it directly over the wound, and then wrapped a bandage tightly around my thigh. Nervous, I hurriedly put my pants back on and cleaned up all traces of the crazy accident so that Mom wouldn't notice anything when she got home.

I was completely oblivious to how fortunate I'd been that day, and even though I'd come to learn that fate had a whole lot more in store for me, it often felt like someone was watching over me.

Medical report from Southern Peninsula Clinic, September 27, 1988:

The accident occurred at 08:30. The Boy says the knife was thrown in the back of his right thigh yesterday morning. The mother didn't know of the laceration until this morning. Examination: laceration down to the Subcutis muscle near the bone of the middle back right thigh, gaping slightly. The wound was cleaned, disinfected, and closed. The mother will monitor for signs of infection and remove the bandage after 12 days if all is well.

Ice and Fire

The knife had just missed my femoral artery!

But soon, thankfully, another more positive male role model timeously entered my world when, in 1987, when I was 8 years old, my Aunt Amelia, one of my mom's many sisters, introduced me to 'The man with the power.' My favorite aunt and I had a very close and special friendship. "Part of you belongs to me," she would joke. "Particularly your big toe." As a child, I took this literally, of course.

'The man with the power' turned out to be a Filipino man named Ed Fernandez, who had been invited to Iceland by the Pentecostal church in Keflavik. Ed was a short, kind man with a very warm and comforting presence, something I was quite unused to. I enthusiastically started karate lessons at the church with Ed, and I always felt happy and safe around him. Even though we didn't speak the same language, I felt a strong connection to him that felt almost supernatural or magic.

You see, for a long time, I'd suffered from terrible, debilitating, chronic stomachaches that nobody could ever explain or diagnose. But, for some reason, in Ed's presence, the ache just disappeared, and, in its place, I felt a deep sense of well-being and ease. He made life feel exciting and positive, and I always looked forward to the stories he would tell us about a man named Jesus. Jesus had lived, and when he died, he actually came back to life and was alive to this day…just incredible! This Jesus, Ed told me, loved even me and unconditionally.

Ed took me aside and taught me the Lord's Prayer, and encouraged me to recite it whenever I felt bad or needed help. "Our Father who art in Heaven"- the prayer that became my lifeline whenever things got tough. I'll always be grateful that Ed came into my life at exactly the right time. Call it serendipity.

One day, after karate, I felt brave enough to ask him if he could come to my house and "fix" my mother. I was so worried, watching her deteriorate by the day... maybe with his healing powers, he could take away her pain, and she wouldn't have to drink ever again! "Only if she truly believes as well," Ed had told me as he and our church director, Kristian, entered our house. That night, I put a lot of faith in Ed's ability to save her and hoped with my whole heart that she would find some peace. That he could give to her what he had given me. But sadly, Mom was not interested, and my hopes were dashed as she sat politely listening and playing along, but really just waiting for them to leave. She would have none of it.

So, even Ed turned out to be a disappointment to me. Even he couldn't fix what was wrong with my mom and my broken family. He did, however, leave me with the prayer that I would carry with me forever. With the absence of a loving and ever-present father in my life and the influence of many harmful and erratic temporary father figures, maybe this "Father in Heaven" was the only father I could really trust.

CPS Report, October 6, 1988:

Brenda and Rikki ended their cohabitation in November 1985. Brenda moved to a Reykjavík apartment with the assistance of the women's shelter. She began seeing a psychologist, who considered her to be mentally imbalanced. She was admitted to Cliff Rehab Clinic for 10-15 days for treatment after attempting to throw herself in front of a bus. Brenda took the children back after treatment until the end of August but then went into treatment again for 10 days and relapsed immediately afterward.

Report, December 11, 1988:

The CPS came to fetch 9-year-old Baldur, but he locked himself in the bathroom and crawled out the window as he would rather be with his mother. It is clear that Baldur sticks up for his mother unequivocally. Her worries and joys are his.

At the end of the day - it was just me and Mom.

3
THE CARETAKER

My mother was born in February 1960 in Iceland's South Peninsula. She was one of fourteen siblings, and as you can imagine, her childhood household was utter chaos!

Mom, with all her strength of character, was always considered different, as she was born with a big, hairy birthmark that almost completely covered her right cheek. This "mark" had made life difficult for her, particularly as a little girl during her school years. Bullying, in those days, was, of course, left unchecked, so my dear mom became a target for relentless teasing and harassment that was left to continue needlessly and unrestrained for years. Mom became used to social exclusion and sadly also suffered from learning difficulties - obviously a natural consequence of all the bullying and alienation. It's no surprise that she left school feeling worthless academically and with an F in self-esteem.

Mom's parents were both alcoholics, so excessive drinking and heightened emotions were common in their home, which should have been her one sanctuary. Like a train station, people came and went, and the constant partying and drinking with guests often led to fighting and domestic issues.

Ice and Fire

Stuck in the middle of this world of addiction, just one of fourteen children, Mom, perhaps inevitably, fell prey to various child molesters who took advantage of the chaotic environment. I'll never forget I was very young when she tearfully told me the story about how she'd been raped in her own home. I ached for her. A deep anger began to grow in my heart, and revenge clouded my thoughts - just another thing to add to my arsenal of animosity. I longed to grow up, be strong and teach them all a lesson.

Mom was my sun, and I was the planet that revolved around her. I remember her sitting on the sofa crying one night, a bottle of red wine and a half-empty glass in her hand and thinking she must have been incredibly thirsty because she emptied the glasses so fast. I sat by her side, hugged her, and tried to dry her tears with the sleeve of my sweater. "Sweetheart," she said, pushing me away, "Mommy just feels bad. That's why I'm drinking wine. It helps me feel better."

Had I been an adult, I might have detected the denial and self-justification hidden in her somber words, but I was only five years old, so I accepted her explanation uncritically as the truth.

I was a little older when she told me about more atrocities she'd experienced during her youth, tears streaming from her eyes in steady, unrelenting streams. I fetched her a roll of toilet paper, which she managed to use up completely, and I watched on forlornly as she stuffed the tear-soaked wads into the empty cardboard roll. The wine bottle was always empty before her tear ducts were. "Baldur, honey, you're my best friend. I've never had such a good friend." My heart suddenly felt heavy - nobody had ever asked me who my best friend was. I was no more emotionally equipped to ask myself that question than I was to listen to the stories of my mother's adult trials and tribulations… but I just did.

Mom, occasionally, did have a quick temper. She'd all at once bite her lower lip, pull her hand back, and bring it smacking down on my cheek.

Every scalding blow she delivered was accompanied by a clear message to me about my worth - "You never do anything right! You're worthless!" I always saw the heartache and regret in her eyes once she realized what she'd done, but the time spent living with Rikki had laid fertile ground in my young heart for the seeds of self-rejection. Much later in life, I realized that I, too, bit my lip just like she did whenever my children tested my patience. But my hand never ever followed.

As a kid, I would sit for long, uncomfortable stretches, waiting for Mom to come home, not knowing where she was or what had become of her. Even though she was usually sad and slept a lot when she was at home, at least I knew that she was with me and we were both safe. Sometimes, Mom hired a babysitter for me, a friendly young woman called Dawn, who'd sit and chat with me and listen to my stories. When Dawn was around, I didn't have to sit by the window, stressed, waiting for Mom to come home.

Ice and Fire

We did have good times though. When Mom was in a happy space, she would often make us her 'Special South Peninsula Caramel.' We, the kids, would watch on excitedly as she let the delicious butter and sugar simmer in the pan for a while and then let us add cocoa to the magic mixture. The whole house was filled with the most heavenly aroma, and a whole eternity seemed to pass while we watched the caramel simmer away on the stove. Once it was ready, she dished it out into bowls and always made a point of giving us all an equal amount to avoid drama. Then we sat, licking lips, our patience tested, as we waited in anticipation for it to cool so that we didn't burn our tongues.

Those nights were just the best! Mom's magical caramel helped us all to forget, watching TV together and laughing as we lapped it up. I wished life could be one non-stop caramel night with Mom.

On one of these fun evenings, Mom decided we were going to take a trip to visit Grandpa the next day, and she announced, laughing, that she'd be "waking us up at the crack of ass" for a visit. So, my siblings and I rushed off to bed and were up bright and early, excited and ready to go! But Mom didn't seem to want to get out of bed. I almost had to drag her out from under the covers until, finally, she emerged, looking exhausted, into the hallway where we'd been waiting hours for her.

"Baldur. Where are my car keys?"

"But Mom," I said, "do we really have to take the ugly old Skoda? It's so embarrassing! Grandpa's is so close - can't we just walk?"

Mom just shook her head, annoyed, and rummaged in her handbag. With a weary sigh, she finally pulled out her keys. "Everything gets lost in this thing!"

So, eventually, we all climbed into the back seat, and just as Mom pulled out of the driveway, we heard a siren. A police car had stopped behind us, lights flashing. Small town.

"Damnit!" Mom muttered as she rolled down the window for the cop. "Brenda," he said. "You know your license has been revoked."

"Yes, I know," she answered with a sheepish look. "I'm just taking the kids to visit my dad, that's all!"

We were all asked to step out of the car, leave it right where it was, and walk home. My mom was not happy!

"Stupid cops. Why can't they just leave us alone!?"

Shortly after this incident, Child Protective Services came knocking again and removed Sophie and David from our home. I stayed on with Mom, shocked and confused. Why were the cops being mean to my poor mom? CPS was evil, stealing kids from their own mothers, and it was their fault that Mom started drinking even more and even started using syringes with needles in her arms again.

At this time, the atmosphere at home became heavy and intense again, and I watched Mom like a hawk, worried that she'd hurt herself.

"Baldur, sweetheart," she slurred, pointing at me, "you're my best friend, my sweet knight in shining armor. I promise I won't do it again. I swear!"

I looked at her, swaying where she stood, and I felt such pity for her. So, I just nodded.

I became my beloved mother's caretaker, a human radar, scanning obsessively for changes in her behavior and co-dependent on her addictive and perilous lifestyle. I was driven by the fear that she'd leave me orphaned, and I carried the burden of responsibility for both her life and mine. I was in it alone, the only child she had left, and I outmaneuvered Child Protective Service's every attempt to take me away from my mom. I'd sneak out the bathroom window whenever I saw them coming, and I learned quickly that if the cops or relatives showed up, it was best to disappear so that I couldn't be taken away from Mom. I'd jump out and hide behind the garage, terrified, until the coast was clear.

Who would take care of her if I was gone?

I learned to anticipate events and find solutions for them fast, but I also learned that nobody, not a single man or woman, could be trusted with my life. I had to look after myself. There was no help to be had.

My siblings were gone; I was the caretaker.

4
SECRET LIVES

As a child, part of taking care of Mom meant sometimes hiding things from her - not only things that I had done but things that had been done to me, as well. I was a fast learner and quickly got used to keeping secrets. Looking back now, it's clear to me why I thought, as young as 7 years old, that I, and I alone, was the black sheep of my family.

To put it lightly, I could be a little crap! Most of the time, my mom didn't have a clue what I was getting up to - especially when it came to my cousins.

I had a cousin who was the same age as I was, and, more often than not, we got up to a lot of mischief. Whether these "awesome ideas" were his or mine, I can't really remember, but I'm pretty sure we were equally responsible for the chaos we left in our wake! On one occasion, when we were seven, we decided it was a brilliant plan to climb the scaffolding around the outside of a half-finished house next to a traffic roundabout on one of the main roads in Keflavik. What an adventure! To us, it looked like a beautiful haunted house from a Hollywood movie, and we just had to explore it!

We started climbing, and about halfway up the wall, I felt an uncomfortable shiver down my spine. Of course, I didn't say anything and just kept on climbing. I wasn't going to give anybody the opportunity to call me chicken! Never! When we finally reached the top floor, breathless, we crawled in through a window and started walking unsteadily on the creaking rotten floorboards inside the house.

"Get your asses down here RIGHT NOW!"

We swung out onto the scaffolding, only to see my uncle, my cousin's dad, screaming up at us furiously, his face as red as the traffic sign next to him. "What are you doing?!" he shouted. Fear gripped me like a vice, and that familiar painful knot of anxiety in my stomach stung me once again.

We hurriedly and, without a word, scrambled down to the floor below to meet our fate, and my cousin's father grabbed his son and pulled him in close, glaring indignantly at me. My heart pounded! He jabbed his index finger into my chest and barked, "Baldur! You're the black sheep of this family. That's it - you're never playing with my son again!"

My heart sank to my stomach, and I just stood there, looking up at him. Speechless.

When I think back on this incident as an adult and a father myself, I can only imagine the fear that must have gripped my uncle when he saw his 7-year-old son dangling from that scaffolding. That was the first time I heard that phrase - 'Black sheep.'

"I suppose I am no good," I thought to myself, as his words confirmed what I already suspected.

After that, I was constantly up to no good, and I started keeping secrets. So many secrets.

Some are darker than others.

Around the same time, I had a cousin who was a few years older than me, and one day, when I was home alone, he paid me a surprise visit. I told him my mom wasn't home, but he just smiled and told me that it was me he had come to see. Flattered and eager to spend time with my cool older cousin, we both strolled into my bedroom to hang out when he suddenly said:

"Hey, Baldur! Can you lock the door? I want to show you something cool."

I did what he asked, only too happy to be part of this exciting thing he was going to show me.

"Baldur," he whispered, looking me in the eye, "have you ever jerked off before?"

I wanted to impress him, but I had no idea what he was talking about, so I just nodded my head. I stood there, trying to act cool, when he suddenly pulled down his trousers. He looked at me casually and then said, "Now it's your turn." I was scared and insecure and had no idea what was going on, but I wasn't going to let it show, so I simply pulled my trousers down too.

I'm not going to get into what happened next, but suffice it to say after it was over, he sat down on my bedroom chair and whispered, "You're not going to tell anyone about this. This is our secret, OK?"

I promised him and kept my mouth shut, but the knot of inner turmoil in my stomach only grew bigger. I knew that it wasn't right, and it filled me with guilt and shame.

After this incident, obviously curious, I started masturbating. I felt ashamed, but at the same time, it gave me a sense of comfort and escape. I also started 'playing doctor' with some of my friends, which, of course, was bound to end badly. And it did. My mother's sister approached me one day, after she had found out from her son.

"It's wrong," she said. "Stop it right now!" I felt overwhelmed with shame and unclean, and that something must be really wrong with me. I complied with my aunt's request and tried to forget about the huge embarrassment, but for a long time, I didn't dare look her in the eye.

My aunt must have told Mom about what had happened because one day, she suddenly started questioning me, "Has someone done something wrong to you, Baldur?"

I pretended not to understand what she was talking about.

"I promise, my darling, you'll never ever have to see the person again, but you have to tell me who it is!"

I wanted to reveal everything but was afraid and ashamed, so I denied it all and played dumb.

"Was it your grandpa, Baldur?"

I shook my head no. My grandpa lived in a little apartment in our backyard - an old garage that had been renovated. I spent a lot of time with him. He was kind, gave me sweets, and was always happy to play with me, but he never did anything inappropriate. I was eleven when I finally told my mom about my 'playing doctor.' She was angry and berated me, and the mortifying shame overwhelmed me yet again. It consumed me and became like a dark, heavy shadow, following me everywhere. Something was definitely wrong with me.

I was the Black Sheep.

Over time, though, I came to understand that the reason I felt such deep shame was because I had, without understanding, responded to my cousin's abuse with pleasurable feelings. He had assaulted me, but his transgression was clouded in my mind by my body's natural reaction. I was 27 when I finally shared this story at the dinner table with my family. I didn't want to cause my family pain or discomfort, but I felt like I would burst if I had to hold it in any longer. Finally, my secret was out. My mom sat at the table, completely silent, but as soon as she'd recovered from the shock, she showed me support, love, and understanding. I sat with her talking, and trauma flowed out of me as if I'd lanced a boil. I felt sick and confused, but in some inexplicable way, I felt lighter and liberated by saying it all out loud.

I realized that I had somehow, over time, come to believe that perhaps I was the offender, but as I related the events to my family that night, my inner critic was, once and for all, silenced. I was the victim, not the perpetrator.

Little did I know that one day, I would forgive my abuser and help others forgive theirs, too.

Little did I know that one day, I would go on to help hundreds of abuse victims.

My secret became my strength.

5
THE KING!

As I grew up, being bullied became something of a way of life for me at elementary school, and group assaults, sadly, just became expected.

Also, to add insult to injury, I had a hideous and embarrassing recurring wart on my nose that, despite repeated attempts to burn it off, earned me all kinds of cruel nicknames.

One day after school, a group of boys from several classes decided to gang up and attack me. They stalked me down outside the school and jumped on me, punching and kicking, as I lay there passively, determined not to show any signs of weakness. After taking a real beating, I suddenly noticed the boys seemed distracted and glanced up to see that my younger cousin, Harold, had come to my rescue and was thrashing out at the group's ringleader. I watched him, and I froze.

At the time, I was living with my mom's sister Bridget and her husband Harold, and when my cousin and I got home that day, I was taught a valuable life lesson. As my cousins watched on, Harold Senior gave me a thorough scolding for not sticking up for my cousin when he had come to my defense. I remember thinking that he was right but couldn't understand why I had just frozen and done absolutely nothing to help him. I would never do that again. From that point on, I always stood up for those close to me, no matter the risk. Thanks to my uncle, I'd learned my first lesson in loyalty.

During this time, I was also frequently sent to live out in the countryside with my mom's sister, Sigga, and her husband, Gunnar. It was a welcome escape. I loved the fresh air and the open space. They gave me hot glazed cinnamon rolls and milk straight from the cow, and nothing was more fun than riding on the back of the Haybale wagon with my cousins at breakneck speeds!

The old farmhouse they lived in was made of wood and built on a concrete foundation, and I often remember that when Sigga did the washing in the evenings, the whole house would rock us peacefully to sleep as the tumble dryer reached maximum spin speed. I always enjoyed being out in the country, even though I really missed my mom and constantly worried about her not having anyone to look after her. In times like these, I'd often quietly recite the prayer that Ed from the church had taught me and ask Jesus to watch over my mom.

One summer, out at my aunt's farm, we heard about a wrestling match that would be held nearby. It sounded like such fun, and I really wanted to give it a try, so my uncle, Gunnar, lent me and his son, Marcus, some wrestling belts. It was an Icelandic Glima competition - a traditional Icelandic wrestling form, where two competitors fight to bring each other to the ground without losing balance, only holding on to the other person's belt. My cousins and I eagerly spent hours practicing with each other, but Marcus soon gave up as it became obvious that I was a lot better at it than he was. The elation I felt when I used all my strength to slam him down onto the grass was amazing! Addictive! Finally, I was standing up for myself. I wasn't a loser anymore!

So, we started attending all the wrestling matches in the countryside. I was filled with exhilaration and determination. I would win every one of my fights and be crowned the 'Glima Wrestling King'!

It all started really well for me; I stacked one defeated, sweaty country boy on top of another with ease and was certain, and perhaps a bit over- confident, that I'd win the title. When the final did arrive, I was completely shocked to discover that my opponent was a girl! A girl more than a head taller than me and by the looks of her, twice as heavy. My hands went clammy with fear, and that critical, nasty little inner voice that I had come to know so well started chipping away at me again.

"Boys shouldn't wrestle girls!" I said coolly, trying to get out of it; just imagine the indignity of being wrestled to the ground by a girl! I'd been so cocky and full of confidence, but in that moment, I just wanted to disappear into the ground.

"Just get on with it!" someone shouted. "She's been wrestling boys the whole tournament!"

There was no turning back now, so I prayed in desperation. I approached the girl and greeted her in the time-honored Icelandic wrestling custom. Then, I grabbed onto her belt, and we assumed the starting position. The whistle blew, and I could already sense the girl's strength as we took our first steps. I knew right then that I didn't stand a chance against her unless I acted fast - I had to hook my right leg behind hers and get her to lose her balance! She was good, but I managed to dodge her maneuvers mostly and stay on my feet. After many gutsy attempts to hurl me to the ground, I finally slid my left foot behind her right one and rammed into her with my full force.

She lost her balance and fell backward. It was over! She was down!

I leaped up and whooped, "Woohooo! I'm the King!" I was triumphant. I'd finally won something!

I enjoyed every second of it.

But unfortunately, not every fight I got into was as controlled and respectful as this one. That same Christmas, I was given a snow racer sled by Mom. I absolutely loved it, and I rushed outside into the snow to slide down the slope behind our apartment block. It was fantastic! The place was bustling with kids, but none of them had a sled as cool as mine. I was dragging the sled up the hill for another run when I heard one of the older boys shout out at me,

"Hey! That kind of sled isn't allowed here!" "Why?" I questioned.

"Just get off our hill and take that sled with you!"

"You don't own this hill!" I yelled back at him, my anger starting to rise. The boy walked up to me, "If you don't get out of here, I'll hit you!"

I hesitated, and before I could blink, the bully started kicking me. I couldn't take it anymore. A sudden wave of confidence rushed through me, and screaming as loudly as I could, I grabbed him in a solid wrestling hold and slammed him into the ground. Squeezing him as hard as I could, I let go with one hand and started pounding him in the back with my fist. "Let me go!" he wailed.

It wasn't until people began to stream out onto their balconies to see what the trouble was that I stopped. I heard my mom shout, snapped out of it, and finally let go of the boy.

"I hate you! I hate you all!" the bully shouted with tears in his eyes.

I watched him run off with his sled, defeated, and enjoyed the thrill of victory. I didn't care. I'd been threatened and attacked and had finally harnessed all of my anger and energy to conquer that threat! I felt big. I felt seen. The dull ache in my stomach had disappeared.

My confidence in my ability to defend myself was slowly growing. On another similar occasion, on a hot summer's day, my friends and I were playing basketball, and I missed a few shots. Suddenly, someone shouted out at me, "You're such a loser. Get off our court!"

Already annoyed that I'd kept missing the hoop, his remark was the last straw! I stared the kid down and told him to shut his mouth, but he just kept going and started walking menacingly toward me.

I saw red.

I ran at him and slammed him straight into the ground.

"That's enough, Baldur!" my buddies shouted at me, as I grew so angry that I started bashing his head into the ground. I felt my friends pulling me off the boy and realized I had gone too far. We bolted, leaving him lying there, unconscious on the court. But I didn't feel guilty. I felt anesthetized. I felt numb.

So, I kept going.

Another day, while visiting my younger cousin Henry, I was bored, so I suggested that we go out together and mess up some seagull nests. He lived next to an uncultivated moorland near the birds' nesting ground. He agreed, and we went into the garage to choose our "weapons." "What is this?" I asked, picking a package up off a table.

"Gunpowder," Henry replied. "Dad uses it in his shotgun."

That caught my attention. "Well, let's take some with us," I said. "Maybe we'll find some lighter fluid here too."

I really enjoyed playing with fire- sometimes creating a makeshift flamethrower out of my mom's hair spray. Henry looked uneasy and hesitated, but I persuaded him to go along with my idea.

I was getting good at that.

We went out into the nesting ground, collected some hatchlings, and sat watching as we covered them in gunpowder, doused them with gasoline, and set them alight. I was mesmerized. Something happened inside me, and I laughed manically as we watched the baby birds burn.

Violence was becoming like a drug. It took the ache away.

For a while, anyway.

6
MY COUSIN AARON

Around the age of ten, I started to realize that anything that gave me a rush of excitement and a surge of adrenalin somehow made me feel good. Made me feel better. Soon after moving into yet another new neighborhood, I made friends with two boys named Simon and Henrik, and we started stealing. Stealing money from clothes in the table tennis locker room, from donation boxes, and from jacket pockets at church. We felt smart and cool. No one would ever suspect us, and we used the money to buy candy, fast food…and sometimes alcohol.

Simon and I would wait outside the liquor store and ask the people going in to buy us a pack of beer. Most people refused and chastised us, but there was always someone who relented.

Then, six packs and all, we would hang out in a little storage room at Simon's house, kitted out with a couch and ghetto blaster, where, as ten-year-olds, we could drink and smoke in peace. It was also during this time that we started experimenting with sniffing White Out fluid. I'd put it in a candy bag and inhale deeply until oblivion washed over me, and the ever-present knot in my stomach disappeared. Our little gang thrived, listening to rap, as we found more and more ways to get high, including huffing lighter fluid and glue. I constantly needed to be doing something because a strong wave of unmanageable misery took over whenever I was even slightly idle.

It was during this time that I became close friends with my cousin Aaron. I loved being with him, and we became inseparable, often tricking people by telling them we were brothers. Whenever I could, I would hitchhike to Aaron's house in Keflavik, and we would go out into the neighborhood alone, free to perform our daring feats and dangerous stunts on the high, slippery cliffs by the harbor. We were two adrenaline junkies, brothers in arms, and it was exhilarating!

Once, in the middle of the day, we were on our way back to Aaron's house when we realized we had been locked out. We tried unsuccessfully to open the window next to the front door, but we were stuck. We could have waited, but we were really hungry and wanted to get inside, so we started to hatch a plan.

"There's a ladder in the backyard!" Aaron said. "Maybe we can climb up and in through the balcony doors. They're never locked."

The ladder, which was lying on the lawn, was long enough to reach all the way up to the third floor. Brilliant! He took the left side and

I took the right, and we started carrying it towards the house. At first, it didn't seem to be a problem, but the closer we got to the house, the heavier the ladder seemed to become. I was 10 years old, and Aaron was 9, and the ladder was made of heavy, sturdy timber. We weren't exactly big, and we started to realize our little muscles couldn't handle the weight. We started to struggle, and the ladder began to wobble.

"I think we need to let go and jump out to the side, Aaron!" I shouted, "Ok…after three! One, two, go!"

I let go of my side and jumped away from the ladder.

Aaron jumped under it.

"Aaron!" I shouted in shock as I heard the thud of the heavy ladder crashing down on my cousin's head! I leaped towards the ladder, and as if possessed with sudden superhuman strength, I lifted it off him. I got the fright of my life as blood was pouring from his head! Normally, I was terrified of blood and would feel sick or run away, but I forgot my fear entirely and carefully helped him, shaking, to his feet.

"Baldur, am I bleeding?" asked a stunned pale Aaron, a look of panic on his face. I looked at him, scared, and didn't really know how to answer. His face was covered in blood. "Just a little!" I replied in a trembling voice, trying not to frighten him. "Come on," I said. "We're going to the police station." Thankfully, the police station was right next to the apartment block where he lived, so we ran as fast as our little legs could carry us, me holding him up.

Ice and Fire

"We need help!" I shouted, pulling open the door.

My little cousin was now drenched in blood. The officers drove us straight to the hospital, and we sat in the back seat together while one of them pressed a strip of gauze tight against Aaron's bleeding head. When we got to the hospital, a doctor came running to meet us, and even he looked worried at the sight of Aaron. Terror gripped me even more tightly when I saw the expression on the nurses' faces as they all rushed him in. Poor Aaron! His skull hadn't been fractured, but the nails in the ladder had torn his scalp to shreds. He got 83 stitches in his head that day, but not even that would be the last time Aaron and I tempted fate.

We carried on with our risky stunts, smoked, stole, listened to Guns N' Roses, and hung onto the backs of cars while they did donuts in the snow. We also gave people a taste of their own medicine, getting into fights with anybody who dared cause us trouble. I made sure that nobody would ever mistreat my "foster brother."

I started to realize that I was getting a kind of kick out of my wild behavior. All of the violence and misbehavior wasn't just about releasing that inner tension; I also started to enjoy the power it gave me over other people. I started to think that Aaron and I were invincible.

We weren't.

One night, I was woken up in the middle of the night by someone shouting.

"Where are they, Baldur? Tell us where the boys are!"

As my head began to clear, I looked up in shock to see my mom and a policeman standing in my bedroom!

"What? Which boys?" I was confused. "Aaron and Julius!" he shouted.

"I'm sorry, I don't have any idea. I haven't heard from my cousin at all today!"

The cop stared suspiciously around my bedroom, asked a few more questions, then left. I lay awake for hours, worried about Aaron and uncomfortable about the cop's threatening attitude towards me. When I woke up the next morning, I ran through to the kitchen to ask Mom if Aaron and his friend had been found.

"They're still missing, my love," she said. "You're going to have to babysit tonight so I can join the search party."

A search-party? It was all starting to sound disturbingly serious. I swallowed, "Can I come too, Mom?"

She refused point-blank and left me standing alone, feeling stressed and useless. I stayed at home and babysat my younger siblings that night, and as the nights piled up and the search party continued without success, I started to feel sick to my stomach. I would sit by the window, waiting for hours, and look at the burn marks on my arm – injuries and scars from the games of chicken that Aaron and I had frequently played with smoldering cigarettes.

The search for the boys was the most extensive ever undertaken in the South Peninsula of Iceland. At its peak, around 250 people took part, combing nearly every square foot of the area without finding any trace of my cousin or his friend. About fifteen divers with submersible cameras searched the harbor; houses and drainage pipes were examined; oil tanks were emptied. Even psychics were enlisted to help, with one of them predicting that the boys were stuck somewhere in an enclosed space. The police ordered a cargo ship that had already reached the open seas to turn around, and every container on board was searched… to no avail.

The weather had been terrible the day the boys had disappeared, but that didn't worry me at all. Aaron and I loved to go down to the cliffs in stormy weather, and we'd become experts at jumping between rocks as the waves crashed down on us. We spent hours taunting the sea, shouting, "You'll never catch me!" The sea seemed to respond to our provocations, and we would often have to run for our lives before a wave crashed mightily right where we'd stood a second earlier. Then, we would celebrate our victory of conquering the elements by sitting inside the concrete shelter high up on the rocks, chatting and laughing.

The very same concrete shelter where a rescue dog finally picked up their scent - but still, they were nowhere to be found. The search continued. I started to lose hope. Maybe one of them had found themselves in trouble, and the other had bravely tried to help, only for them both to be snatched up by a giant wave and swept away. Tears streamed down my cheeks. I couldn't bear the thought that the sea had prevailed. How could this happen? How could my best friend be taken from me?

The search lasted three weeks; then, it was called off. My excruciating sense of loss was kept alive by the hope of finally finding Aaron. For years, every time I saw a blonde boy with long hair, my heart would skip a beat, only to be met with bitter disappointment. The sorrow of missing my best friend spread through my chest like a web, making it difficult to breathe at times. Nobody took the time to talk to me about it; nobody took the time to listen.

How was I supposed to live without Aaron?

7

THE DEATH OF LOVE

Report from Child Protective Services, April 1991:

Baldur and his younger sister, Sophie, show obvious signs of neglect as the result of unsatisfactory living conditions and abuse that are impossible to ignore. Baldur exhibits a charming personality on the surface but also shows signs of obstinance and deceitfulness. The siblings' behavior can be clearly traced to neglect due to their mother's alcoholism, ongoing relationship difficulties, and unacceptable living conditions.

To make matters worse, around the same time, Mom had started drinking again and drinking more. I could always sense the slightest changes in her. Up to three days before she even picked up the bottle again, I'd started asking her to breathe in my face so I could check whether she was drunk. I was always stressed, constantly analyzing my surroundings and her demeanor. She grew more distant and distracted and also started acting really strangely.

One afternoon, she came to pick me up in the car, and I noticed she seemed tense and agitated - sort of highly strung. That's when I started to realize she was taking drugs as well. Amphetamines, I was sure. Over time, things got even worse, and I started finding syringes and white powder in little bags in her pockets. I felt abandoned and defeated, and I just wanted to run away and teach her a lesson.

Then, Mom met Brian. In rehab. Once again, another man who proved to be an appalling role model. He moved in and made absolutely no attempt to connect with me, so I didn't bother talking to him either.

There was also only one bedroom in our small apartment, so, like it or not, we all had to share it - me, Mom, and Brian. I felt ok with this arrangement at first because they told me that they were going to get sober together, and I really hoped Mom would maybe finally do it with his help. But it only became a nightmare for me, as time and time again, I would be woken in the middle of the night by my mother and Brian having sex.

Can you imagine anything more excruciating for an adolescent boy? Very soon, I had had enough and completely lost my patience! I would sit up in my bed, get dressed as noisily as I could, and storm out of the apartment. The first few times, they came running after me dramatically, but eventually, even that stopped. One late night, having been woken up by them yet again, I stood up and shouted furiously:

"That's it- I'm leaving!"

Mom pleaded with me. "I'm so sorry, Baldur! Honey, wait! Please don't do this!"

Ice and Fire

"Ugh, just let him leave, babe," Brian piped up from the bed.

Stunned, I ran out to the garage, and I wept. I felt completely unloved, and my stomach ached as my tears drenched my face. When I was done, I pulled myself together, went back inside, and went to sleep.

One evening, though, when Mom wasn't home, I was sitting in the lounge with my cousin Denni when Brian walked in. He stood in the doorway looking at us, annoyed, for what seemed like ages, then finally asked if we were going to go to bed. When we said no, he rolled his eyes, dug into his pocket, and asked us if we had ever smoked hash.

"Um…yeah," we replied, acting cool.

"Well, if you smoke anyway, I couldn't be bothered waiting for you to go to bed," he said. "We might as well just do it together."

He then took out a gram of 'Black Afghan,' as he called it. He lit up his bong, and we all got so stoned that the night ended in huge fits of laughter. Something else changed that evening, too - my relationship with Brian. We were on the same level, now…or so I thought.

Brain and Mom were always breaking up and getting back together. Brian suffered from depression, so I was always careful to be quiet whenever I came home from school because he was usually asleep in the bedroom. He had a tendency to throw temper tantrums if I disturbed him, so I got used to tiptoeing around at home. Mom tried to defend me, but one day, he completely lost it. I had woken him up by mistake, and he walked into the kitchen and started fuming.

His voice boiled over with contempt as he lashed out at us "I hate you!" he spat at us. "You're both miserable losers! Get out of here!"

I got scared, even though Mom was with me. It all felt way too familiar.

We ran out of the kitchen, and just as we reached the hallway that led to the front door, I caught a glimpse of the knife that he'd thrown at us. It had just missed us and was stuck fast into the dresser by the front door. We ran out as fast as we could, jumped into the car and drove away.

The next day, Brian and Mom promised me that they would stop everything and sober up, but as usual, that soon went up in smoke and Mom ended up back in the hospital. I ended up back out in the country with my Aunt Sigga again. But this time, it didn't last long. After a few days, Sigga sat me down with a serious expression on her face.

"Baldur, my dear," she said. "I'm afraid I have some bad news." "What's wrong?" I asked so quietly it was barely audible. "Honey, your mom jumped out of a window at the psych ward." I stared at her in silent disbelief.

"And she's broken her back." I swallowed back the tears.

"She's in the hospital," she said quietly. "Hopefully, she'll stop drinking now."

I was speechless and could feel the tears running down my face. Sigga wrapped me in a tight hug and tried to console me. Why on earth would my mom throw herself out of a window? Why didn't she just walk out the door? Would she be able to walk again? Would she be paralyzed? Later, I found out that Mom had been declared incompetent and admitted to the psychiatric department for 48 hours for substance abuse. She told me that she'd only been trying to escape to go on a drinking binge and had underestimated the fall.

I was getting really frustrated with being pushed from pillar to post, so in February 1991, at 13 years old, I left the countryside and I went back to stay with my aunt Amelia. There were two families living in her single-family home, so it was always bustling with activity, but I soon realized that something very bizarre was going on in the house. I started overhearing strange conversations between my two aunts at night.

Apparently, my late grandmother was "communicating" through one of them. They would transcribe these mysterious messages and write them down, discussing their meanings late into the night.

Some of the things I remember overhearing were that Grandma had said we were no longer allowed to eat meat, we were forbidden to cut our hair, and we also had to change our names. My two cousins and I were given the names Faith, Love and Hope.

I was told that I was 'Love' - a reincarnated yogi with an extremely important purpose in life. My cousin, Grace, Amelia's daughter, had also started to behave strangely; she became withdrawn and began talking in riddles. I had no idea what to say or do, so I just went along with it all.

One day, driving around with my aunts, my Aunt Amelia suddenly declared passionately, "I am the alpha wolf!" I was in the back seat listening, and I suddenly remembered a movie that I had watched recently, where the wolf was a kind of God.

"I've got it!" I shouted excitedly.

"Got what, honey?" Aunt Amelia asked.

"You're God!" I exclaimed proudly, "If you're the alpha wolf, and the wolf is God… then you're God!"

"He's got it!" she whispered conspiratorially to her sister in the seat beside her. "Baldur, honey, you're right, but you must never tell anyone!"

Then, she winked at me and started howling like a wolf out of the car window.

As time passed, the situation deteriorated, and we were sworn to secrecy on all sorts of things. Sometimes, at Amelia's command, we all had to run out to the car and drive around so that "The Evil" wouldn't catch us. Aunt Amelia explained that there was a metaphysical war going on, and this war was usually waged at night. My cousin Grace was put in charge of the escape route and had to sit in the front seat and direct the driver. Grace was clearly very upset and scared. I was terrified when I saw what she went through trying to save us from the evil demons that were trying to steal our spirits. As Amelia explained, if evil won, we would all be without souls, merely husks.

Things came to a head one morning when I woke up and noticed that everything was strangely quiet in the house. I looked everywhere and couldn't find anyone. I started to worry, so I opened the front door and went out onto the deck. Suddenly, I saw the cars racing down the driveway. They slammed on their brakes, and Grace opened her car door and came running towards me, arms outstretched, tears streaming down her face.

"I'm so sorry, Love! You are dead! We forgot you last night and the house was burnt to the ground. Your spirit was incinerated."

I stood on the sidewalk in my underwear and t-shirt, staring at her. Confused. What had happened? How was I supposed to live without my spirit? I turned around and went back into my room. Who was I supposed to be now? I was no longer Love.

Love was dead.

Report from Social Services Board, Seal Bay, June 15, 1991:

"Baldur has been staying with Brenda's sister Amelia, who resides in Keflavik. Keflavik CPS received a report that conditions in the home were extremely unstable, and eviction was imminent. The visit revealed an extremely bizarre situation within the home. Amelia appears to be no longer of sound mind, and there is evidence that she has been using drugs. Brenda has retrieved her son, Baldur. It has been proposed that Baldur undergo a drug test, as the boy also appears to be in a peculiar state."

8

HIGH SCHOOLING

After this very strange departure from reality, I went back to school but was still struggling with depression and malaise. I couldn't focus on anything and found my thoughts very often revolving around death. I had no interest in the death of other people, only my own. I also constantly thought of my cousin, Aaron, and I so longed to feel that strong friendship and togetherness again. I disappeared into my mind, and my reality felt bleak and miserable.

I discovered there were many ways to rid myself of the constant nagging anxiety. The White Out fluid in the green candy bag was one way that whisked me away into oblivion in a matter of seconds. Mom caught me in the act one afternoon, lying on my bed with the green bag over my nose and mouth.

"What on earth are you doing?!" she screamed and slapped me with the back of her hand. I stared into her eyes, totally empty inside and almost unconscious from the inhalants. I sat motionless as she yanked the bag away from me and left the room, swearing at me. "Is she supposed to be scolding me?" I thought, baffled by my mom. That evening, she lectured me angrily about huffing inhalants. People were left braindead and drooling in wheelchairs. I'd heard all this before at school: ineffective fear tactics if you asked me. I didn't care anyway.

Drugs weren't as readily accessible in those days as they are now, so I had to be very resourceful. Hash was my favorite - all of my worries became so trivial that I could just laugh at them. I had started using very early in life, and from the very beginning, my appetite for drugs was voracious. I saw humor in everything when I was high, no matter how I'd felt in the minutes before. At the same time, my drinking escalated, and I'd become a frequent guest in the school principal's office due to behavioral problems and insolence. I was eventually expelled from school, but in some inexplicable way, though, I was able to get people to side with me. Even my mom! I generally managed to get myself out of trouble without much more effort than a lie and a smile.

So, I was sent to complete tenth grade at a boarding school in Akureyri, in the north of Iceland. I wasted no time getting myself into all kinds of trouble. There was no way I was going to let anybody control me, let alone some teachers way up in the sticks who didn't know the first thing about real life. Not the life I was barreling head-first into, at any rate. I didn't last long and was soon expelled and sent back to Reykjavík.

I moved back to Keflavik with Mom. No matter where we fled, trouble seemed to find us. Or maybe we just brought it along with us. On the weekends, I'd go down to Keflavik's main drag, with all its bars and clubs and accompanying debauchery. My habit intensified, and my repertoire of drugs expanded. I also had a girlfriend named Annie. I'd met her while working in a fish factory in the summer. She was a charming girl who was one year older than me. Annie and I hadn't been together for very long when I found out that she had cheated on me. I felt my heart shatter into a million pieces, and my anger boiled over. She ended our relationship and started a new one with the man she'd slept with. Rejection consumed me, and I locked myself away from everyone. My mom sealed that sentence when she let me know that when she'd met Annie, she had told her that I wasn't "boyfriend material" anyway. I was speechless.

Alone now, my friends and I drank and snorted amphetamines every weekend. We had also all just received our driver's licenses and were experts in driving around the city like lunatics. Racing, intoxicated, down Keflavik's main street one snowy evening, we heard a sudden loud thud and I saw a pedestrian go flying across the hood of the car.

"Man! You hit a guy!" I shouted, scared. My friend, Ivan, just floored it and peeled away, tires screeching, and we ended up stuck on the pavement, having crashed into a fence.

"Get into the passenger's seat! Quickly!" I shouted. He was too drunk to make a run for it. Panicking, I scrambled behind the wheel, got the car down off the sidewalk, and sped away. I drove into town, and we disappeared into a friend's house to avoid arrest. Once we were in the clear, we all started to laugh. Nothing changed after that, though…we kept burning the candle at both ends. Whenever I was drunk or high on the way home from a party somewhere, the cops almost always stopped me. I was finally starting to live my own life, my own way, but they were always there.

Just like my stupid feelings - taking every opportunity they could to smother and control me.

9
STARING AT COFFINS

In a significant twist of fate, when I was 17, my grandparents (Rikki's mom and dad) invited me to go abroad with them.

"Where are you going?" I asked, curious and excited. I'd never left Iceland before.

"To Norway first, on the ferry," my grandma said, "then we'll drive over to Denmark to visit Aunt Anna."

Anna was Rikki's twin sister, and they both lived in Denmark at the time. I thought about it for a millisecond, then said, "Yes! Why not!?" There was nothing good happening for me here at home. It didn't matter, anyway. I was the Black Sheep. Plus, I'd always dreamt of going to Christiania, a Mecca for hash culture in Copenhagen, in which, by this point, I was deeply immersed.

Our trip started well, but my habits didn't change. Even on the ferry over, I spent almost every evening getting smashed in the boat's bar.

"Why don't you just come down and sleep, honey?" my grandma would encourage me. Grandma really cared about me. She always had such a knack for getting me to do the right thing. Our short time in Denmark went well, but a few days before it was time to go home to Iceland, my grandparents approached me, asking if I wanted to stay in Denmark.

"Anna's found a job for you!" she smiled. "You could live here, with them, while you get back on your feet."

Ah...so there had been a reason behind the trip, after all! They were trying to protect me. My grandfather had obviously heard about my run-ins with the cops back home. He was a police lieutenant, after all.

So, I started working with Anna in Slagelse, a city of just over 40,000 people on the island of Zealand. What they neglected to tell me was that the job was making coffins! I had to laugh - not your typical first job!

Anna's husband Matthew was really supportive and kind and even got me into the boxing club in town. I was thrilled! Now, I could finally start practicing the sport I'd only read about in books. I loved training and learning the techniques, and I practiced hard. There was nothing I enjoyed better than getting rid of all my pent-up aggression in the boxing ring after work.

At first, I lived with Anna and Matthew. They were good to me, but they were conservative, so I had to hide my addictions from them. I relied on narcotics to numb the depression that had started again after my move to Denmark. The news that there had been a memorial service for my cousin Aaron in Iceland didn't help at all.

Ice and Fire

In fact, it hit me full force, and the constant ache in my heart and the heavy knot in my stomach became almost unbearable. I hadn't been allowed to take part in the search for Aaron and Julius, and now I was stuck in Denmark and couldn't even attend their memorial.

Once again, I sensed how out of place I felt; I clearly didn't belong in my family, or anywhere else for that matter. On top of it all, I'd heard the news that my mom was off drunk somewhere again.

My lust for life quietly waned, and the only recourse I could find was to simply shut down. Life wasn't worth living, anyway, and to make matters worse, I was just a burden to everyone no matter where I went. It'd be a relief to everyone if I just left.

I wrote a suicide note to my family, mainly discussing arrangements and how I wanted them to play Bob Marley's 'Redemption Song' at my funeral. I wrote a short goodbye to Mom, explaining my decision to end my life. I sat, weeping as I wrote, but felt relieved once I had finished. In my mind's eye, I saw myself hanging from the rafters. I stood up, inspected the ceiling beam that crisscrossed the room, and slid a chair underneath it. I fetched my leather belt and tugged on it with all my might to make sure that it could hold my weight.

I stood on the chair, pulled the belt taut around the ceiling beam, and stuck my head into the noose it formed. I hesitated on the chair for a little while, closed my eyes, then I carefully stepped down off it.

I hanged myself. I was 17.

I remember feeling the hard leather tighten around my throat before everything went black. I lost consciousness. I'd kept the chair close by, close enough that I could easily have reached out and grabbed it with my feet, but I had no desire to stop what I'd started. All I wanted was to sleep forever.

The next thing I knew, I was awake and lying on the floor. I didn't know if it was the impact of the fall that brought me back, but I just sat there in a daze. I was even incapable of topping myself. How big of a loser could I be?

I saw the belt lying on the floor next to me and gave it a closer look. There was a straight cut right across through the thick leather.

Completely linear and sharp, as though I'd been cut down. It suddenly occurred to me that maybe Anna or Matthew had found me and cut me down. Shaking, I walked out into the hallway and went downstairs.

Nobody was home. I looked around the room and at the belt again to see if I was missing something. It was impossible. Someone had to have stepped in.

I was shaken and changed forever. Maybe someone, or something, was watching over me. Maybe there was a purpose to my life after all.

So, I kept going.

I decided to learn to speak Danish, and I was quick to pick it up. I became fluent in just over three months. I made an effort to get to know Sebastian, my employer and the owner of the coffin business. I often made rounds with him after work, delivering coffins. We stopped at the shops along the way, and he bought us 'Fernet Branca' and 'Tuborg Gold' beer, and we drank together every day. Sebastian lived alone in a house in front of the workshop, and since we were spending so much time together after hours, delivering our products all over Denmark, he invited me to move in with him. So, I moved out of Anna's house and into his. It was comfortable and a bit of a relief because I would no longer have to keep up the charade of sobriety every day.

In return for his hospitality, he told me that all I had to do was make sure his wine cellar was full. Fair swap, I thought! I took his card to the wine shop in Slagelse and kept him well-stocked at all times. I was very interested in learning about business, so I asked him, "How come you've made it so big in the coffin business?"

He told me that his only competitor in town had sold a coffin to a family, and the bottom had broken. It dropped out just as it was being carried, dumping the body and rolling onto the ground in front of all the mourners. Inevitably, the reputation of the business took a massive nosedive. Even though I obviously found the incident horrifying, there was something so ridiculously comical about it that we both laughed our heads off. Then laughed some more.

I kept pushing to stay positive. Sebastian loaned me his delivery van so I could get to boxing practice, which I loved. Gradually, after learning how to box, my overblown reactions to altercations changed. I was learning to fight like a real fighter without seeing red or losing my self-control. I enjoyed my social life and loved the beer culture in Denmark, and it certainly didn't hurt that it was easy to get my hands on drugs, which were of a much higher quality than the ones back home in Iceland.

But I was still depressed. I was lonely.

As the days turned into months, I developed the habit of standing in the workshop and staring into the coffins. I imagined myself lying inside of them and felt a strange sense of relief. I didn't find my thoughts macabre but rather soothing. It was as if I could hear the hoarse whisper of death as I stood there, the coffins staring back at me.

I did have a close call one night after a couple of hours of drinking with Sebastian and the cleaning lady who worked for him. She needed to drop her car off at home, so inebriated, I followed behind her to drive her back to the party. As we were crossing over a bridge, I felt a sudden smashing impact as she rear-ended me, sending me careening into the side of the bridge. The impact dislodged a large, sharp piece of iron that came flying towards the side of my car, where it stuck. When I looked back on this incident, I realized that if I'd hit the pole a fraction of a second earlier, the iron wedge would most certainly have pierced my abdomen. I suffered a heavy blow to the chest that made it difficult to catch my breath, and I felt a stinging pain in my ribs. I managed to slide myself out from under the seatbelt with difficulty and climbed out of the smashed car. The cleaning lady sat in her car, staring into space, in obvious shock.

The police arrived quickly on the scene and took me into their car for questioning. They handed me a balloon and told me to blow into it. I tried, but the pain in my ribs made it very difficult.

"Blow properly, Icelander!" one of the cops sneered. They passed insulting comments in Danish and kept going at me until I was able to push through the pain and sufficiently fill the balloon. Obviously intoxicated, we were both taken to the station for blood tests.

I was deeply ashamed when Sebastian found out.

"You'll lose your driver's license, kid," he said. "And you'll have to pay for the car because the insurance won't cover this." But he was kind and didn't seem to take it too seriously. There was a brand-new van in the driveway a few days later, and he stopped talking about it.

I was summoned to the police station, my head hanging low, only to be told that my license had indeed been revoked and I'd have to pay a month's wages in fines for driving under the influence. My blood alcohol concentration measured 0.125.

"Who's going to be at fault for the accident?" I asked.

"Not you. She ran into you, not the other way around. Besides, her blood alcohol was 0.185. Higher than yours."

I breathed a deep sigh of relief. I felt awful for her, but for once, I wasn't the main culprit.

And I had escaped death. Again.

Not my only accident. It would happen to me again with a friend in Iceland, Johan, who was as crazy as I was at the time. One afternoon, he and I were on our way into Reykjavík to pick up drugs. He drove his old Honda like a lunatic, as usual, going well over a hundred in traffic. As we flew past an entire line of cars, a Ford Econoline suddenly appeared, careening straight towards us.

"Slow down, man!" I shouted. "There's no way we'll make it!"

Ice and Fire

But Johan did just the opposite and stepped on the gas, staring straight ahead as cold as ice. My entire body stiffened. I was sure we were going to collide head-on with the larger vehicle speeding towards us. I held my breath and closed my eyes, and the first thing that came to mind was the prayer Ed had taught me. When I heard a loud screeching noise, I just knew that it was all over, and we'd hit the Ford. My body went limp and I couldn't move so much as a finger.

But when I opened my eyes, I realized that somehow, inexplicably, we'd made it. We had escaped completely unscathed! Once again, I had the strange sensation that someone was watching out for me.

For a boy who spent his time making coffins, it was an absolute miracle that I didn't end up in one.

10

A LIGHTBULB MOMENT

Not long after arriving in Denmark, while living with Sebastian, I made a new friend, Karsten. He was the same age as I was and just as passionate about our mutual drug habit. Karsten and I often made the hour-long trip into Copenhagen to pick up decent hash in Christiania. It was awesome! I felt as if I'd died and gone to heaven. We bought all the hash we needed in Christiania and then went into Copenhagen city center to party our days away. Our only responsibility - to make sure we caught the last train home.

After a short while, we decided to live together, and we found an apartment directly above the train station. No longer having to hide our secret habit, we could party nonstop. I'd already started developing a reputation in the bars around Denmark for stirring up trouble, and I started noticing that people were avoiding me out on the streets. I was ecstatic! I was finally the untouchable badass I'd always wanted to be, and I didn't cut anybody any slack if they even so much tried to mess with me. I was finally a grown man.

One night, I was out of town along with another Icelandic guy I'd met called Gunni. As we were walking in the street, minding our own business, three boys headed menacingly toward us, clearly out to pick a fight. They stopped right in front of us.

Knowing what was about to go down, I muttered to Gunni, "You take the one on the left; I'll take the other two."

There was no answer. Gunni had legged it. The 3 guys smirked at me and moved closer.

"I'll just have to take all three of you then!" I said in Danish and took aim with my fists.

All three came at me at once, but with a stroke of luck, I was able to send one to the ground instantly with a jab straight to the jaw. Crack! One of the others lashed out at me threateningly and kicked at my legs. I stepped back and sent him falling to the ground to join his buddy. They kept going, but by the time I was finished, all three of them were horizontal.

I frequently found myself in situations like this, and the following weekend, I even broke my hand while punching someone. The bone was so damaged that I could barely make out the shape of my fist when I inspected it the next day. I hurried to the hospital, and the doctors told me that they wanted to insert a pin in my hand to help re-set the shattered bones. I politely declined, saying: "It's not like I'm about to start playing the piano or anything like that." But I did manage to persuade the doctor to prescribe me some strong opiates under the pretext of pain management and wasted no time in opening up the capsules and emptying their contents into my beer so that they'd start to work instantly. As always, I needed the buzz.

Times could be tough, but I was really starting to enjoy my life and work in Denmark. Later that summer, I went on a holiday to Iceland. On the flight home, I started feeling sick, and by the time I got home, I realized I was actually in withdrawal from the painkillers, so I drank alcohol to help alleviate the symptoms. I stayed in Keflavik, and as Mom was in a halfway house at the time, I used every available opportunity to get high.

A few days after I got home, I received a difficult phone call.

"You need to get here immediately, Baldur. Your dad has had a stroke."

My birth father had been transported by medivac from the boat he worked on to the intensive care unit at the National University Hospital. Even though my dad and I rarely met and hardly had a relationship, I was still very shocked and worried. I rushed to the hospital and met my dad's family properly for the first time, all gathered in the waiting room. I mostly knew them all only by name, except for my dad's wife, Gloria. I had once lived with her after one of my many expulsions from school.

A short while later, the doctor came in to meet us, his expression grave.

"The procedure he's about to undergo is very risky; we don't know whether he'll survive."

I felt my stomach tighten into a knot. Why was this affecting me so badly? I hardly knew him at all.

"He's such a fighter," someone remarked. "If anyone can survive this, he can!"

I couldn't sleep that night. I hoped and prayed to God that he'd recover. The procedure thankfully went well, and amazingly, Dad survived the operation. Sadly, though, he was never the same afterward. I said goodbye to my dad's family, and they promised to keep me updated about his progress.

I decided to stay in Iceland. I couldn't think of returning to my life over in Denmark while the situation at home was so dire - Mom in a halfway house and Dad ill in hospital. After he was moved to a recovery ward, I would visit him. I tried to talk with him, but he mostly remained silent, and I received limited responses in return. It was hard and uncomfortable. I wish I'd visited more and tried harder, but I didn't.

Things got worse for me after that. I partied hard and lost the plot, trying to numb the pain. I took more and more drugs and drank more and more booze. Something inside me just snapped, and one terrible night, I decided, again, that it was time to make my exit. I ended up in hospital, having my stomach pumped after an overdose. I was miserable and in a lot of pain.

Medical report, University Hospital, June 17, 1997:

Baldur Einarsson

18-year-old Baldur ingested Nobligan 10-20 pcs, Panakod 20 pcs, Parkódín forte 2 pcs, Panodil 30-50 pcs, Voltaren Rapid 30 pcs, and a half liter of moonshine. He has been under a lot of strain lately; his father was recently diagnosed with a stroke, and his mother has been in a halfway house and relapsed last night. Baldur ran into his mother drunk at a night club, became very distressed and returned to his mother's sister's house. His aunt found him shortly after he'd taken the medication and brought him to Keflavík Hospital, where his stomach was pumped, and he was administered charcoal. He has recently arrived back from Denmark, where he was reportedly using amphetamines and hash daily.

Then, the shame set in again. Now, everyone knew that I wanted to die. Why couldn't I just die? Mom was devastated and tried to talk me into either going to rehab or checking myself into the psych ward. I had a lot of visitors because she'd called everyone we knew and asked them to stop by, probably to prove to me that I had people who cared. I sat there embarrassed and feeling small. My uncle Eli came to visit me one afternoon, and unlike everyone else, he just chastised me:

"What were you thinking, doing this to the people who care about you? You can't let yourself act this way, Baldur!"

As uncomfortable as it was to hear his words, they were the ones that affected me the most.

Ice and Fire

One day, while I was still in recovery at the hospital, I reached into my gown pocket. An artist friend of mine, Christian, had visited me a few days before and written a prayer on a piece of paper for me. I was so desperate to get high again that I even considered just quitting and falling off the wagon intentionally. I thought about faking spasms or a seizure so that the nurses would give me another hit of Benzodiazepines. I looked at the little folded-up piece of paper and made my way down to the hospital chapel. I figured that if God was anywhere, he'd be there. I knelt in front of the altar. I didn't have any faith that this prayer could save me, but since I had next to no hope whatsoever anyway, I thought I might as well give it a try.

I knelt in front of the altar and started to read the prayer when an eerie gust of cold air crept down my spine.

I felt strangely alive. I kept reading. Could this actually be working?

"You're just in withdrawal," my analytical inner critic replied.

I dropped my head, and in that very second, the electricity in the building went out, and the lightbulb hanging above my head exploded with a loud bang! I stood up in shock and immediately broke out in goosebumps. Despite the darkness inside the chapel, I felt an immense power, an almost tangible light within me. And a vibration so intense that I forgot all the time and place.

"What are you doing here?" I heard a voice.

The janitor came rushing into the chapel.

"Praying," I said, breathless.

"What happened to the lightbulb?" "I don't know. It just exploded."

I was shivering as the electricity suddenly came back on. The janitor stared at me strangely for a moment, then started cleaning up.

I walked past him in silence and returned to my room.

I sat down on the bed and stared ahead of me. An intense feeling of well-being blanketed me. I was exhausted and wanted to sleep, but the inexplicable, infectious strength that had filled me kept me awake, warm, brimming with joy. My anxiety was simply gone. What amazed me the most was just how easily it had happened. It seemed so simple. I had prayed a single prayer in very weak faith, and it was as if one light had been switched on inside of me while another had exploded on the outside. It had required no effort - just a prayer. I was stunned!

Something inside me had changed.

After the hospital stay, I went to a different rehab facility where I made an interesting new friend, Alfie, also a recovering addict. We got on brilliantly and had many of the same interests, including my newfound fascination with prayer. We spoke for hours at a time, and my faith was growing. We eventually decided to spend our combined energy on starting up a charity to help others. We would call it 'Needle's Eye'. Our plan was to start a mission and take Bibles into Vietnam. I also started attending worship services at the church regularly and found myself dancing in the front row and singing my heart out. I'd always loved to sing.

Yet, underneath it all, I was still struggling with myself. My addictions, my lustful thoughts, my self-esteem issues, my family. My fear of rejection by others - especially the pious people who attended service –was also still very much alive and well. Everyone else in the church seemed so perfect; I was certain that I was the only one there who struggled with vices and demons. I couldn't imagine that any of them experienced the profane thoughts that I did.

I would look around me and often witness people burst into spontaneous tears whenever they experienced God's presence. I realized then that it had been a year since I had last cried; I'd been completely frozen inside. I wanted to cry too, so after a meeting one day, I sat on the steps leading up to the altar and decided to pray to Jesus. To help me cry. I closed my eyes, and I saw an image of Jesus. I felt shame. I looked down at his feet and found myself reaching out towards them. I didn't dare look up; I felt so unworthy.

Then, tears began streaming down my cheeks and onto the floor. I just wept. I wept so much that I had a hard time stopping. I don't know how long I sat there, but gratitude spread through my body as I let down all my defenses and my heady feeling of worthlessness vanished. There on the steps.

I'd finally found something worth fighting for.

I started working as a peer mentor in the summer of 1998 when I was 19, and we went around warning young kids about addiction and the dangers of drugs. I worked with Peter, a 16-year-old boy I'd met in rehab, and we held each other accountable for our sobriety. The best part was that we had a purpose! Others could learn from our mistakes, and nobody had to suffer like we had. I loved it. I also, happily, started to feel some good consequences of my newfound faith at home with my family, especially in my relationship with my little sister, Hanna.

Hanna (Mom and Brian's daughter) was the hero of our family. She was a brilliant football player, destined for great things at a national level.

Little Hanna was a funny contradiction in many ways. On the one hand, she was tough as nails, which she displayed clearly on the football pitch. She was an intense defender- no one could get through if Hanna was in front of them! But she was also very soft and gentle. Always very warm and caring to everyone, Hanna had a special place for me, her big brother. Her rock. Looking back at photos of her when she was excelling as a footballer in her childhood years, I noticed she was often holding onto her teddy bear - her 'good luck bear' that she took along to her matches. A tough, tenacious defender on the football pitch, a sweet, loving child off it.

While I was working in peer counseling, Hanna would often come to me and ask me to pray for her. She experienced pain from leg injuries on the football pitch. She had so much faith in me. She would conscientiously close her little eyes, hold my hands, and then look up at me with admiration. She always felt "so much better" after every prayer.

I was helping the people I loved. Things were finally going well. Alfie, my partner in the charity, and I were still planning our exciting trip to Vietnam. I couldn't wait! The sheer anticipation kept me going. We had our passports ready, and we had bought several hundred Bibles to hand out when we got there.

One evening, I was over at Alfie's, and I instantly sensed a change. He was avoiding questions, and he just didn't seem himself. As soon as I heard the tell-tale rattle of a pill bottle, I immediately knew what was going on. After all, my childhood had earned me a master's degree in seeing through addicts. He'd relapsed. He left the room and ducked out to the bathroom, and I decided to look in his pockets. Sure enough, there were several bottles full of diazepam.

"I saw the pills in your pocket, Alf," I confronted him. "I'm just taking them for anxiety," he said sheepishly.

It was over, and I left his house completely shattered. He was just a junkie, trying to delude himself. The journey was canceled, and our yearlong dream of preaching in Vietnam was over. My friend and confidant had relapsed, and I was alone once more.

There seemed to be nothing on the horizon. I tried to keep the faith and kept up my counseling work until one day, when I'd been going to church for about a year, one of the older women working at the church approached me.

"Baldur, it's time for you to make some changes so that you can be sanctified."

"What does that mean?" I asked curiously. "You need to start coming to church in a suit."

"Ok, but I like coming in light clothes so that I can dance." "Baldur, you have to do this!"

I felt frustrated again. "Are you sure God cares what I wear?" "Yes," she said caustically, "God wants you to wear a suit!"

She looked me in the eye, and the familiar old cloud of rejection blocked out every ray of light I'd been holding on to. Hiding my feelings, a worthless good-for-nothing again, I smiled at her, said goodbye…and left the church.

I wasn't good enough. I didn't fit in. I just didn't wear the right clothes.

11
CROSSING THE LINE

Not long after leaving the church, when I was still sober, I met a girl named Andrea. I fell for her, hook, line, and sinker. Andrea was very popular with the boys, so I felt very special when we started dating. She had chosen me. We were deeply in love, and I moved straight in with her, but living together didn't go quite as planned. I was young and insecure and, because of that, became extremely controlling. Controlling over the cooking, the house, where she went, and the attention she gave to other boys. I was totally unlovable - why would anyone want to stay with me? I knew I was messing up, and my special relationship was hanging by a thread.

Then came the bombshell. Andrea was pregnant. "I want an abortion."

There it was again, that old familiar feeling. Rejection. She was rejecting my child, a part of me. I knew I wasn't good enough for her.

I relapsed immediately and started taking uppers on the sly, sneaking around and hiding it all from her. Instead of trying to salvage the relationship or fight for the tiny life growing inside Andrea, which I wanted to save, I opted for my most familiar escape - drugs. Andrea asked me to come with her to the hospital for the abortion. I sat with her, watching while they did a scan, feeling useless and ashamed. After all, it was my fault.

The scan revealed an ectopic pregnancy. "It would have had to have been terminated anyway," Andrea said numbly. I held her hand as she lay weak in the hospital bed. I tried to do right, tried to show her the support she deserved, but my mind was a million miles away…obsessing over the drugs hidden in my pocket.

"Where's the bathroom?" I asked the nurse.

As soon as I was inside, I locked the door, and hands shaking, took the little bag out of my pocket. I hurriedly did a few keys, making sure the tap was running loudly so that nobody could hear me snorting. I still wasn't satisfied. I looked into the mirror -

"Look at you, taking it up the nose in a public toilet while your girlfriend is lying there after losing your baby."

I took out the bag again and had more. My hair stood on end as the high kicked in and electrified my whole body. Finally, my annoying pangs of conscience vanished, and I went back into the ward to Andrea. I sat down next to her, and my palms instantly broke out in a cold sweat as the intoxication reached its peak. I was careful not to touch her or hold her hand so she wouldn't suspect anything. She looked at me, intense emotional distress in her eyes, and I felt nothing.

Nothing but the high.

When I said goodbye to her at the hospital, deep down, I knew it was for the last time. I had room for nothing and no one else in my life. I locked that sad little box and threw away the key.

I had already given the AA twelve-step program a try, but I was still desperate to find a way out of the mess I was in, so I decided I would give it one more feeble attempt. I couldn't handle being sober long enough for even one meeting, so I went high on drugs and missed almost everything that was being said. Stoned, I wandered up to the rostrum at the front of the room and talked to the group about how I'd used it while I was at the hospital with Andrea, how lost I felt, and how I'd lost all faith in myself.

A man named Palmar, a well-respected, long-sober twelve-stepper, took the stage as soon as I had finished and reprimanded me.

"You shouldn't be talking about using when you have the floor, son." He shamed me with an accusatory stare. I sat there, silent, feeling sick to my stomach, wishing that the earth would just open up and swallow me whole. Nothing was working. Church hadn't worked, and I clearly didn't belong in the twelve-step program. This pompous idiot knew nothing!

There was clearly only one solution- I would throw myself completely into my habit.

I stood up and left.

I got in my car and went straight to my mom's old friend and dealer, George. I knew he would take me in, and I could get a fix in peace without any arrogant know-it-alls butting into my personal business.

After a few days there, I was in terrible shape, so I asked George to get me a couple of sheets of Mogadon, a strong Benzodiazepine, which he did. The darkness was smothering me again, and even though there was an opening for me at a rehabilitation center after a few days, I saw no point in going. All I could think about was falling gently to sleep and not waking up again.

I couldn't get sober, I couldn't make a relationship work, and nobody loved me. Simple. So, I went home and took the pills he gave me. Mom was off somewhere, probably getting drunk, so I had peace and quiet. There was only one right choice, for my own good and everyone else's.

"Wake up, Baldur!!" I heard Mom's distant voice. She was shaking me hard and slapping me repeatedly on the cheek. She'd come home to find the pill packaging on the floor and me lying unconscious in bed. I came to for a few minutes but was still only semi-conscious when she got me to the ICU at the local medical facility.

Ice and Fire

I was beyond agitated. All I wanted was to get out of there and get my hands on more drugs because I couldn't bear the thought of the comedown. It terrified me. My family desperately tried everything they could to get the doctor to declare me incompetent and keep me overnight, and in the end, they succeeded. I heard them out but refused to be admitted unless I was given the drugs that I needed to curb the effects of the comedown. It didn't take me long the next day to convince the psychiatrist I'd suffered a bout of temporary insanity. He watched me dryly as I tried to pull the wool over his eyes but concluded that I wasn't a suicide risk and let me go. I was relieved to be free because now I could go and get myself some stimulants. I didn't like a mellow high - my preferred poisons were uppers. They discharged me with a prescription for the sedative Librium. I was to take this for two days or until I could get back into rehab at the hospital.

I promised him I would.

I went straight to George's place and started shooting up. I'd always been afraid of needles and had never done it before, but I had never been so desperate either. I sat on George's couch. He took out the powdered amphetamines, put a little bit on a spoon along with some water, held the spoon over a flame, then placed a cotton ball on the spoon and drew the mixture up into a syringe.

"Take off your sweater."

I did what he said, then held my arm out. "Clench your fist a few times…"

I pumped my fist to make my veins more visible; then he stuck the needle into my arm. It stung as I watched some of my blood swirling up into a mixture in the syringe. He pushed down on the plunger, and there it was again.

That kick.

It was wild! Every hair on my body stood on end as my eyes widened and rolled back. I was free…lost in space and time.

I started getting hold of other drugs to keep up with my constant demand. It was an expensive habit, but I never had any trouble selling and found out quickly that I had a knack for that. I threw myself into the abyss head-first. This was now my modus operandi - I used as much as I could get my hands on until I couldn't use anymore.

In the spring of 1999, at 20 years old, I shuffled into Vogur rehab center, utterly depleted. My counselor called me in for an interview:

"Baldur, what do you think of going into long-term treatment?"
"How long?"

"A year."

Ice and Fire

I thought it was a completely ridiculous suggestion! I had just turned 20, barely even old enough to buy cigarettes and booze, and I was supposed to go into long-term rehab. Come on!

"I'll think about it."

I didn't. The next day, I went straight to the nurse's station and announced that I was checking myself out. I didn't belong in any long-term treatment program. I didn't have that big a problem.

I walked out of the hospital, took a deep breath, and in that moment, looking out at the city, I made the decision to become a criminal.

I crossed a threshold.

I knew then that I belonged in that world. I was accepted there. I could even be respected… and I could make a living dealing. I would sell drugs and always have an ample supply for myself. The perfect plan.

I devoted myself to my new task wholeheartedly, as I always did with everything I undertook in life. I always went all the way.

This time though, it would have terrible consequences.

Part Two

12

THE DEBT COLLECTOR

It was 1999.

Surveying our territory, I stopped the car on the crest of a hill overlooking the mountain pass into Reykjavik. Christopher, my partner in crime, handed me the speed, and we indulged in another line.

At just 20 years old, my new life as a criminal was taking shape. Christopher, my friend and co-conspirator, was built like a brick wall, roughly the same height as me and tough as nails. Together, we were a crazy, reckless duo, often teetering on the edge of sanity. A potent and very dangerous combination. I first met Chris in a twelve-step recovery program when we were both sober. Now, a world away from that reality, we were peddling narcotics for a dealer named Andre.

I was fiercely committed to being excellent and determined to establish my own niche in this new world. We were ruthless, and when addicts failed to pay their debts on time, we would simply break into their apartments, ransack their belongings, and, more often than not, administer brutal beatings. Our number one priority was always to stay one step ahead of the cops, and we used violence, or the threat of it, to dissuade anyone from ratting us out to the authorities.

And it worked.

With adrenaline and amphetamines constantly coursing through my veins, I felt more alive than I had in a long time. I thrived on the excitement of the constant chase and above all, the respect it earned me. I had finally found my spot in the world. I was the one calling the shots now, and I had loyal friends who would protect me through thick and thin.

Stan was one of them, and he was quite the character - foolishly fearless and wild. He had already done prison time by the age of 15, so he was a bona fide experienced criminal when our paths finally crossed. Stan, Chris, and I became a formidable trio. Mostly completely out of our minds on amphetamines, we felt invincible, which often led us into very dangerous situations.

In a break from our usual routine, one night, the three of us decided we were going to try and pull off a robbery. We had received a solid tip from a friend who was an insider, and we were strapped for cash, so we decided, why not? At around 11 pm, we parked our car around the corner from the shop. We stood, balaclavas over our heads, armed with bats, lurking behind the back door. Our "amazing" plan was to knock out the last employee to leave and then get to work. I was completely wired; my adrenaline was through the roof, and we had mere seconds until our target emerged. Then suddenly, out of nowhere, two sets of car headlights approached from the opposite direction and illuminated the darkness around us, completely exposing us.

The job was blown. We scurried away into the night, frustrated that the burglary had been bungled but mostly relieved that we hadn't been nabbed.

I had been there before, and there was nothing more excruciatingly uncomfortable than spending a night in a holding cell. No matter how high I was initially, it all wore off during those 24 hours of confinement, and that was insufferable. In those dreaded hours, my muted, angry, hypercritical conscience would always make a surprise appearance, taunting me and inevitably ending in me needing to take an even bigger hit of drugs to silence that belittling, suppressed inner voice.

"Aha, there you are... Black Sheep."

Our near misses with the law were just the tip of the iceberg, and the brutality was only just beginning. One summer evening, Stan and I were strolling through downtown Reykjavik, and as we entered a park, my eyes locked onto Frosti - one of the unreliable junkies who owed me money and never bothered to answer his phone. He didn't owe me that much, but this chance meeting gave me the opportunity to set a precedent and make it abundantly clear that disrespect would never be tolerated.

"Hey, Frosti - when are you going to settle up?"

"Baldur! Please! I'll do it right now," he whimpered.

"You're too late, loser. You should've answered your phone!"

"I didn't know you'd called!"

"Oh, so now you're going to lie to me too, huh?" I bellowed, my frustration suddenly boiling over.

I was just doing my job, ensuring that Frosti paid the price for his irresponsibility. He needed to suffer so that I didn't look a fool. I grabbed him by the hair and forcefully slammed his face into an iron park bench. As Frosti rebounded, Stan caught him like a ragdoll and locked his grip around Frosti's throat, allowing me to finish what I had started. I inhaled deeply, raised my fist high, and delivered a powerful punch to Frosti's cheek. The sound of something cracking echoed as my fist connected.

Then, I started to pummel him- blow after blow after blow.

"You're going to kill him!" Stan yelled.

I froze and released my grip on Frosti, who crumpled to the ground, battered and bloodied. I grabbed his arm and mercilessly stomped down on it with my heel, feeling his bone snap beneath my shoe, all while rifling through his pockets and wallet, taking everything we could.

We unceremoniously tossed Frosti into the bushes like a sack of sand.

"Nobody messes with us!" Stan shouted, laughing, as we slammed the car doors shut and sped away like lunatics.

Later, I found out that I had shattered every single bone on the right side of Frosti's face. His cheekbone, orbital bone, and jaw were all broken, his skull fractured, and his right arm severely damaged. How was I supposed to feel? It had had the intended effect, and the news of our ruthlessness spread like wildfire throughout the city. People now understood that paying us on time was the wisest course of action.

After that, life returned to its usual grim routine. We peddled drugs for profit, and crime and brutal punishment became our routine daily grind. One night, as Stan and I cruised around during our usual rounds, my phone rang. It was Simon, one of our regular customers, a young member of an up-and-coming motorcycle gang. He wanted drugs, specifically speed. We drove into Reykjavik, to his basement apartment, parked outside, and waited. When Simon eventually stumbled out of the house and made his way toward us, it became abundantly clear that he was very inebriated. He lurched his way into the back of the car, reeking of alcohol and trouble.

"I need some speed, man, "he slurred.

Eager to just get rid of Simon fast, I handed him the speed, and already heavily intoxicated, he wasted no time taking a hit right in front of us. But then, instead of paying up and leaving the car, he just sat there, annoyingly goofing around, talking loudly, and causing trouble. The tension in the car escalated rapidly, and it didn't take long for a very irritated Stan to reach his breaking point.

"Listen, mate," Stan raised his voice, his anger simmering. "I'm going to count to ten. If you're not out of this car by then, I'm going to pop you one. Got it?"

Stan knew that Simon could easily leave before he reached ten, but he had already made up his mind - he was going to rough him up regardless. This was often the way things played out with Stan.

"One... two... three... ten!"

On the count of ten, Stan's fist connected with Simon's face. Crack!

He reached into the backseat and unleashed a barrage of punches, kicks, and blows until Simon tumbled out onto the street, limp, bleeding and battered. We hit the gas and sped away from the scene, chuckling to ourselves. He had asked for it. He should have known better.

A few days later, a quieter Simon called me, claiming he had the money he owed. Without a second thought, I drove over to his basement apartment to collect my dues, but as soon as I walked in, I could sense the palpable tension in the air.

Eight hostile-looking men in leather jackets confronted me at the door.

"So, Baldur, where's your buddy Stan?" one of the older men hissed, obviously out for revenge.

"How should I know? I'm just here for the money Simon owes me."

"There's no money, mate, and you're not leaving until we've had a little chat with your friend Stan. Get him here... now!"

I stood there, my mind racing through various escape plans, but it was clear that the only realistic way out of this trap was to call Stan. So, I dialed his number.

"Okay, I'll be there," he said.

As expected, when Stan arrived, he was not alone. He had brought Chris, Andre, and a few other strong arms with him, all grinning from ear to ear with malice. Tension crackled in the air, and I couldn't help but love the electrified atmosphere. We stood shoulder to shoulder, unyielding and cold as stone, while the biker gang demanded reparations for Simon's beating.

But there would be no reparations…only bloodshed.

Chris started the onslaught, landing a ferocious punch that sent one of the bikers crashing against the wall and crumpling to the floor. It was on! The little basement apartment erupted into chaos, and one by one, we knocked the bikers to the ground, showing no mercy.

"Hey, Stan!" one of the gang members taunted before lifting a large shovel and swinging it straight into Stan's face, knocking him back, dazed. Laughing loudly, the leather-clad bully prepared for another blow, but Andre intervened, saving Stan's face but breaking his arm against the shovel. Another brutal swing of the shovel into Stan's bloodied face sent him reeling around wildly… the drugs he'd taken were the only thing keeping him upright.

I watched in amazement as Andre, fueled by rage, wrestled the shovel away from the maniac, dragged him out into the street, and bludgeoned him with it.

Stan finally toppled over, his body limp and concussed.

It was over. We were all driven to the ER by Andre's girlfriend. Andre needed treatment for his broken arm and injured hand, and Stan needed urgent care for his severe concussion.

Later that evening, we left the hospital with unfinished business and a burning desire for vengeance. It was not over. We were on the hunt.

While I drove, Andre made a cryptic phone call.

"I'm coming to pick you up," he told an unfamiliar voice on the other end of the line. He directed me to a house in Reykjavík. We parked outside, and a giant of a man emerged - tall, dark-skinned, and massively built.

His name was John Stones. I had no clue who he was, but we were on a mission, and we all had one target in mind - the shovel-wielding maniac from the brawl. We found out his name was Samuel, and after a brief search, we found him outside a café in downtown Reykjavík.

"You're coming with us!" Andre screamed furiously at Samuel as we dragged him, kicking him into the car.

We sped out towards an isolated part of town, down by the ocean. Our excitement and thirst for revenge fueled our high as we all clambered out of the car.

"So… this is our guy!" John Stones taunted menacingly, eyeing Samuel and holding the very same shovel Samuel had used on Stan.

Samuel lay face down on the ground, shivering.

"Look me in the eye, you freak!" John barked aggressively, driving the shovel into Samuel's terrified face. Samuel screamed and reluctantly met the gaze of the hulking madman towering over him.

"That's right. Now open your mouth, idiot!"

Shaking and pleading, Samuel complied, his mouth open, as John Stones jammed the edge of the shovel deep into his gaping jaw and forcefully pressed down on the handle, driving it in deeper. I couldn't help but flinch; the air was thick with agony.

"Now pay up!" Andre shouted.

After a lot of screaming and desperate pleading, Samuel made a few phone calls and managed to scrounge up some cash. We released him for just short of $2500, then tossed him into the car and drove him to the drop-off point, where a man was waiting for me with the ransom money.

Just another day at the office.

This was my new world. People knew who I was, and my reputation was growing. I heard the whispers of my name, and my ego was fed. I basked in the attention.

I was the debt collector.

13

CLASHING WITH COPS

I quickly learned during this tumultuous time that 'always one step ahead' could only hold true for so long. As my career in the seedy underbelly of Reykjavik's drug scene progressed, so did my encounters with the law. Trouble had an uncanny knack for finding me, even when I wasn't actively seeking it.

One fateful afternoon when I was 20 years old, I was hanging out with my friends in a downtown video arcade when a troublemaker started mouthing off to me, provoking me and pushing my buttons for a reaction. I had dealt with guys and situations like this before, but on this occasion, I felt an overwhelming surge of anger, and all I could envision was shutting him up with a swift punch to his face.

I started with reason.

"Listen, man, nobody cares, so please just shut it!"

But my attempts to shut him up just fell on deaf ears. He kept going, inching closer and closer to me and getting right in my face as people began to stare. I finally convinced him to step outside with me, and as soon as we were outdoors, the guy pulled out a knife.

Ice and Fire

Seriously? Give me a break, I thought. I was well-versed in Icelandic self-defense laws, and I knew that I could legally defend myself if my attacker was armed with a deadly weapon, which he clearly was. Whatever happened next, he wouldn't be able to press charges, and I had every right to teach this moron a lesson, which I really wanted to do. A crowd of witnesses had gathered, and, to make matters worse for him, a group of reporters had huddled just behind the district court, waiting for someone to arrive for sentencing under police escort. The thug stood glaring at me like a madman, wielding the knife in my direction, and the entire incident was captured on camera. Say cheese! He finally lunged at me with the knife, and I quickly disarmed him, wrestling him to the ground as he screamed in agony. Judging by his shrieks and the way his leg buckled under the force of my kick, I must have hit the right spot.

When the police arrived on the scene, they were intent on arresting me until I explained that the man lying on the ground had attempted to attack me with a weapon. I showed them my wound, a minor knife graze and, of course, the weapon he had used. The reporters joined in, confirming that he had come at me with the knife and that they had captured the entire incident on camera. Later that evening, Icelandic news channels reported the breaking story:

"Knife-Wielding Assailant Subdued in Downtown Reykjavík!"

I had unwittingly become something of a local hero, a twist of fate that my friends found both ironic and very amusing.

That was the one and only occasion that I found myself on the right side of the law. Our run-ins with the cops became more and more frequent, and my friends and I became so sick of them busting us that one day, we decided on what we thought was a cunning plan to exact revenge on them. We had heard rumors about a secret police holding facility on the outskirts of town, so, high and ready, we drove out there in the dead of night, turning off all the lights in our car as we approached. We checked for any signs of life inside, then sneakily made our way to the entrance and pried open the door. We had hit the jackpot! We snooped around the empty building and discovered, to our delight, numerous files containing a wide array of drugs sealed in plastic, as well as some small bags of hash. We laughed and joked around as we lit up a joint and snorted a few lines of our enemies' "stash" in their "secret lair." We then pocketed everything we could carry and stashed it away in our hideout. We were never caught, and the authorities had absolutely no inkling that we had anything to do with the heist. Always one step ahead.

Despite my ongoing conflict with the police, I never got into confrontations, either verbally or physically, with them. My rebellion took different forms, like recruiting people to steal things for me in exchange for drugs. I loved the thrill of knowing that my possessions were all stolen goods and the police had no way to prove it. I also had people hold onto the drugs hidden in my apartment, typically clients who owed me money. This arrangement allowed them to reduce their debts to me by taking ownership of the confiscated drugs.

The key to success in this game was to remain tight-lipped during any questioning. To keep my mouth shut. It was like a strategic chess match for me.

They knew. I knew.

I just had to make sure to keep outwitting them.

The only time I failed, sadly, was with my younger brother. At 14, my little brother David came to visit me from Denmark. I was entrusted with looking after him, and my mom had asked me to plan something fun for him because he looked up to me and was excited to spend time with his cool older brother.

When David arrived, my sole focus was selfishly just on getting my next high, so I took him along to my friend's apartment for a smoke. He sat with us, smoking weed and getting stoned, and after a while, obviously off my head, I made the decision to let him try some speed as well. There were drugs scattered all over the apartment, but in my altered state of mind, I thought it was all under control. I was wrong. Looking back, it's clear to me that I had absolutely no appreciation for how young David actually was or the impact that all of this would have on him. However, whenever I shot up, I made a point of going into the bathroom. I didn't want to do that in front of him.

We hadn't been at my friend's apartment for long when suddenly, there was a loud banging at the door. It was a police raid. We were unperturbed; this was nothing new to us. The cops never left us alone. "Stand still! Don't move!" they ordered harshly as they rushed into the apartment. We knew the drill, so we let them handcuff us as usual. But then I saw them heading toward my brother, David.

"Hey! Wait, wait! He's under 18. You can't handcuff him! You need to call his mother and let her know what's going on!"

My plea fell on deaf ears.

I watched with simmering anger as they manhandled and arrested my little brother, whose only "crime" was being near me. I kept quiet, understanding that it was futile to argue with the police. Another 24 hours in the holding cell. I knew the game; I just had to ensure I didn't have drugs on me and keep my mouth shut during questioning. They led us all, including my little brother, into a cell, and when I protested that it was illegal to detain him, they still ignored my protests.

I loathed them for it.

Poor David was subjected to very harsh questioning and interrogation under "suspicion of smuggling drugs from Denmark." In their relentless case against me, the police worked him over. A 14-year-old kid with neither his mother nor a lawyer present. They were beyond determined to pin something on me, but I refused to give in, keeping my silence for the customary 24 hours.

The next day, they put David into emergency custody at a Child and Family Affairs facility. They contacted my mother, and finally, they released him.

I had clashed with the police once again, and this time, I had come out on the losing end. But they were the crooks, and in my drug-fueled arrogance, it never crossed my mind that I might be responsible for putting my brother in such a traumatic situation. That I could possibly be the problem.

That I was the common denominator.

14

THE CRACKS APPEAR

The summer that followed my brother's visit was marked by escalating violence and continued chaos. Stan and I constantly spurred each other on, pushing our boundaries and ensuring that anyone who showed us even the slightest hint of disrespect would suffer severely for it.

One morning, already very high, Stan and I pulled up at a drive-through window at a bus station to buy cigarettes. The woman working at the cash register asked us to move forward to the next window, and just as I was about to do so, the driver in the car behind us honked his horn loudly and what I thought was aggressive. He had pushed my buttons.

I turned to Stan, agitated, "I'm going to teach this asshole some manners, man!"

Without a second thought, I sprang from the car and stormed over to confront the guy. Stan got out of the car and ran straight to the window where the checkout lady stood, eyes wide, frozen in complete shock.

"Close the window for a sec!" Stan instructed her. She complied, obviously terrified.

Ice and Fire

I tore open the door of the other driver's car.

"Who do you think you are, honking at me?"

Completely stunned, the man tried to apologize, but before he could even get a word out, I started to pile on the punches. Bam! Bam! I held him by his shirt collar and struck him hard under the chin, knocking him out cold so that his head slammed onto the horn with a loud, continuous blare.

Three guys in the backseat watched me in terror, so I flung open the back door, growling, and started to swing at them. Then, suddenly, I heard Stan shouting,

"This knife won't go through his leather jacket!"

Stan was inside the car on the passenger's side, trying to stab the guy in the front seat with my tiny little pocketknife. In the madness of the moment, I burst into laughter at Stan's words. The manic chaos charged me like a drug.

The driver lay unconscious with his head still on the horn, which was blaring across the parking lot. We knew we had to split, so we jumped back into our car and raced away before the cops could catch us, our car doors still hanging open.

We were the crazy new kids on the block, and our reckless and irreverent behavior and the trail of destruction we left behind us began to attract trouble that we hadn't anticipated. On one occasion, one of the scary head honchos on the drug scene at the time, 'Siggy Tattoo' phoned me out of the blue. Fresh out of prison for an assault charge, he was livid about what we had done to Simon (the drunk idiot who hadn't paid up).

I was undeterred.

"Where do you live?" I asked insolently. "We're coming for you, you coward!"

We managed to track him down, but when we arrived at his place, all the lights were off, and nobody seemed to be home. We pounded on every door and window, but it was clear that good old scary Siggi had either fled or was in hiding. That was that! We heard nothing more from him and our message had been crystal clear. He may have clung to his past glory and notoriety, but we were unimpressed by tales of old has-been underworld heroes.

A few days later, at the end of the month, while waiting in line at the bank, I happened to spot Gunnar - another sneaky regular customer who owed me money, of course. I sidled up next to him in the queue, wearing a sly grin.

"Don't even think about causing a scene, my friend," I whispered menacingly.

Ice and Fire

We approached the teller together. Gunnar swallowed. "He wants to close his account, please," I said, smiling. The teller glanced at Gunnar, who nodded.

After a few uncomfortable moments of silence, the teller handed over the money, and we left the bank.

Outside, I locked us both inside an ATM booth and called the guys to tell them that I had finally found the elusive Gunnar. He owed us a lot of money for amphetamines and had repeatedly lied his ass off to me on the phone, making promises to pay and never following through. I could never understand how people like him could lie to my face, knowing that we lived on a tiny rock in the North Atlantic where no one could hide forever. They must have thought we were stupid.

When the guys arrived, we grabbed Gunnar, tossed him into the trunk of the car, and drove him to a national park on the outskirts of town for some peace and quiet. We opened the trunk, and the onslaught began.

"I swear I was going to call you Baldur!" he wailed, looking up at us, terrified.

"Stop lying, and at least be smart about it, man!"

I reached into my gym bag, pulled out my deodorant, and shoved the rollerball end into his mouth.

"This should keep you from lying, you idiot," I shouted.

Judging by the look on his face, I could tell it tasted absolutely disgusting. We yanked him out of the trunk, removed his belt, and told him to pull down his pants and get on the ground. We cracked the belt with all our strength across his bare ass repeatedly as he writhed in agony. The malice inside me swelled with every scream. I believed my actions were totally justified and, at the same time, an outlet for all the anger and hatred that had built up in me over time.

"Pull up your pants and turn around!" I said to him coldly.

I lit a big fat Cuban cigar.

"Take your shirt off."

I wasn't done. I looked him in the eye while he removed his shirt, and then I sat, straddling him so he couldn't move. I puffed on the cigar until the glowing ember reached a good size, then, slowly, I bent over and put it out, sizzling, on one of his nipples. I could smell his burning flesh and continued to stare him dead in the eyes as he squirmed in utter agony.

I had become almost totally indifferent to the suffering of others if I could convince myself they deserved it. It was as if I saw myself as a guardian of justice with a duty to make people respect our values and principles. When it came to physical confrontations, I had a different code. I'd let the other person make the first move. I excelled at taunting people with just enough contempt to provoke them into attacking me. Strangely, I couldn't understand why I was frequently the target of aggression. It didn't matter how many times this happened; I'd always respond with unrestrained violence. I had developed an uncanny ability to visualize how I could overpower everyone around me, instantly spotting potential weapons in the room if things got physical. Violence consumed me, and I had become addicted to it, even more so than drugs.

I vowed never to be a victim again, and I would stop at nothing to avoid that old feeling of helplessness. I was no longer a naive little boy; I had found my voice, and I could stand up for myself.

Whenever my friends and I got extra coke from our drug sales, we always performed a fun little ritual. We'd cook it up in a pot, draw the solution into pre-filled syringes, and store them in the fridge, like ice lollies. The coke was extremely potent, and I quickly realized that no matter how much we had, it always disappeared in the blink of an eye. We were junkies. On days when we were focused on selling, we settled for speed, occasionally mixing in a touch of cocaine, which we jokingly called our "work fuel."

Once, I decided to experiment with Clonazepam, but the experience was so horribly disturbing that the morning after taking it, I woke up completely disoriented and feeling ill. I reached my hand out for a hit of cocaine, only to find it was missing. I tore my apartment apart in a frantic search; I knew it had to be somewhere.

Then I suddenly remembered that my friend Harold had visited my place the previous night before we had gone out to party.

I called the boys. "Harold stole the coke!"

"Nah, man! Are you sure?"

"Yup, dead sure. Let's set him up!" We called Harold over.

"Where's the coke?" I demanded. "What coke?"

"The coke you stole!"

"I didn't take any coke!" he insisted, playing confused.

I didn't believe him for one second, so it was time for a confession. We bound his arms behind his back with rope and led him into the shower stall. We then placed a rag over his face and started pouring water into his nose and mouth through the cloth. Waterboarding. There was no confession, but we kept going between his shouts and struggling.

Eventually frustrated, with no answer, we locked him inside the dark bathroom alone and pounded threateningly on the door at regular intervals to intimidate him. Nothing was working, so, eventually, I broke down the door, grabbed him by the throat and crotch, and threw him across the room, only to fall onto his bound arms. I was determined that I would eventually break him, so the torture continued for several hours. Only when Stan's dad arrived at the flat did he manage to convince me that it was pointless and to just give up and release Harold.

Exhausted but still furious about my coke, I reluctantly cut the ropes around his wrists and let him go.

A few days later, as I sat down to breakfast, I poured myself a bowl of cereal, and there it was - the very same baggie of cocaine I had accused Harold of stealing. Hidden away in a breakfast bowl in my kitchen cupboard. Well, well, well! I thought to myself. He had been telling the truth all along. A pang of guilt washed over me. He didn't deserve what we had done to him, but it was too late to change anything now. I heard from a mutual friend that it took Harold months to recover from our violent interrogation, both physically and emotionally.

Harold had paid the price for my addiction to brutality, but he wasn't the only one.

Around this time, my mom was given an apartment by the city council, and, for convenience, I decided to move in with her. I was still using intravenously every day and was neck-deep in all kinds of crime, so it suited me pretty well. My dodgy, fast-paced lifestyle inevitably caught my mom's attention, with the constant stream of people coming in and out of our apartment, my room filled to the brim with stolen goods, and me, perpetually off my head on one drug or another.

"You need to go to rehab, Baldur! Please!" she implored me one afternoon.

Give me a break! Life was great. Rehab was absolutely out of the question for me, and my mom's own behavior was hardly perfect. I couldn't understand why she was lecturing me.

About a week later, my mom called me, whispering down the phone in a total panic. She and my 14-year-old sister, Sophie, had been attacked and robbed at our home. I rushed home, panicking and beyond furious. I knew who it was and exactly what it was about.

"What's your plan, Baldur?" my mom asked, worried.

My inner fury was so intense that I couldn't hear her. I just left the house without replying, gathered a group of neighborhood guys, and drove into the city. To avoid being seen and recognized, we parked the car around the corner from the bar where the culprits were hanging out. We all walked into the bar, spotted the gang, and without hesitation, one of my friends grabbed a heavy red ashtray and hurled it straight into the face of the man who had robbed my mom and sister.

As soon as it connected, chaos broke out, and we sprang into action, thrashing the lot of them, my hatred and animosity finding release with every blow.

However, instead of easing my mom's stress, this violent retaliation only exacerbated her worries about me, and she seemed to be growing increasingly anxious.

A few days later, I got home to my mom standing in the kitchen, systematically emptying the cupboards by smashing plates and tossing dishes shattering onto the floor at my feet. One plate after another soared through the air and smashed as she screamed and shouted curses at me. When she'd finally finished smashing everything she could lay her hands on, she picked up a large, sharp kitchen knife and held it in the air shakily, breathing heavily.

"What are you doing, Mom?" I shouted, not knowing what had suddenly come over her.

Without hesitation, my mom looked at me, took the knife and made a deep cut lengthwise from her wrist all the way up her forearm. Blood sprayed everywhere around the kitchen. A horrible cold chill ran down my spine.

"What have you done!?" I panicked. She fixed her gaze on me.

"If you're going to continue down this path," she shouted, "I don't want to live!"

Panicked, I grabbed a dishcloth and wrapped it tightly around her arm, applying pressure to stop the bleeding. I called for an ambulance as fast as I could. Mom just stood there, staring at me with deep anguish in her eyes and tears streaming down her cheeks while we waited for help to arrive. I rushed with her into the emergency room and stayed with her until the doctor arrived, then hurried back home.

When I opened the front door, I saw the bloody shards of glass and dishes scattered across the floor and hallway. I couldn't breathe. I spotted the knife on the floor, sickeningly covered in my mother's own blood. A heavy wave of nausea ran through me as if something inside me had shattered as well. In a panicked daze, I ran into the bathroom, tore off my clothes and got into the shower. As the warm water cascaded over me, my tears began to flow, and I curled into a ball on the shower floor, sobbing and trembling uncontrollably. It was as if I had completely lost control over my body and my emotions. I was in a state of extremely severe shock, and seeing the bloody knife on the floor like that had triggered my deep-buried fears and terrors of my childhood.

When I eventually calmed down, I got dressed, rolled a joint, and then got to work on eliminating any trace of the traumatic incident. I picked up the shattered glass, wiped the blood from the knife, and meticulously scrubbed every single surface of blood. I was determined to keep this horrific incident hidden from anyone and everyone. I steeled myself and decided it was best to forget these useless thoughts and feelings altogether.

It hadn't happened.

15

VENGEANCE IS MINE

My phone rang. It was Mom. It was about a month after her incident and hospitalization, and I sensed by her tone that something was very wrong. I stopped what I was doing and rushed home immediately. As I hurried into Mom's apartment, I saw my little sister, Sophie, sitting at the kitchen table, head bowed, with tears streaming down her cheeks. My sweet Sophie, usually quick-witted and fearless, was shivering, crying, and at a complete loss for words.

"What's wrong, Sophie? Please, tell me what happened. You don't have to be scared. I'll take care of it; you know I will," I reassured her.

She couldn't speak.

"She's been raped," Mom said, her voice filled with anger. "Some guy took her to his place and then dumped her afterward, like trash."

My temper surged, and I felt my hands begin to shake as I clenched my fists. My knuckles turned as white as the linoleum tabletop.

"What's this bastard's name, and where does he live?" I growled out before I could even breathe, my voice trembling with fury.

Sophie just cried, and I wrapped her in my arms, shivering. "Shouldn't we report it?" asked Mom.

I looked at my little sister sitting there in pieces. She'd already suffered enough, but Mom was livid.

"Iceland is for Icelanders!" Mom suddenly shouted out, her anger boiling over.

At that moment, I understood. The man who had raped my sister was a person of color or someone my mom saw as a "foreigner." Her own mother had instilled this racist belief in her. Unbridled fury erupted inside me. I sat with Sophie, gathering all the information I could, and then I called the crew, not revealing the reason yet because, at the time, we were convinced that the police were monitoring our calls.

"Sophie's been raped," I told the guys when we met. "The guy's name is Mike, he's black and a foreigner. He hangs out with Icelandic girls and then takes advantage of them. It's time to teach this asshole a lesson he'll never forget."

The atmosphere in the car on the way was so thick with tension and rage that you could almost cut it with a knife. We parked the car out of sight and started our search by knocking on the doors of a couple of basement apartments, to no response. Finally, we approached a third door and knocked.

Ice and Fire

A young Icelandic guy answered the door, and I pushed my way past him inside.

"Is Mike here?"

"No," he replied. "there's no Mike here."

We walked into the living room. Two teenage girls and a black guy were sitting, watching TV.

"Are you Mike?"

"No." he said irritably, "my name is Shaun."

We asked him a few more times, but he just kept repeating the same answer. I didn't want to punish the wrong guy, but as we left, a feeling of uncertainty gnawed at me. Then it hit me; I had the guy's phone number. He had called Sophie the day before, and she had given it to me.

I paused, took out my phone, and dialed the phone number. A phone rang inside.

Surprise surprise! It belonged to the guy who had called himself "Shaun."

Without a second thought, I ran straight at him and started pounding his face ferociously. The girls freaked out and froze on the sofa.

"You're not going to get away with what you did to my sister!" I screamed. "You f...ing rapist!"

The girls started screaming and crying.

"Show me your ID's so we know where you all live!" I shouted as I pummeled him.

When I was finally done, I looked at Mike lying on the floor in a pool of his own blood, his face swollen. I grabbed him by the hair and lifted him up onto the sofa, and pulling his head back, I whispered, "This is for my little sister Sophie... who you raped!"

I turned my old Nokia phone around and forcefully jammed the antenna into the contusions on his face, bursting them open. Only when I was covered with his blood did I finally decide to stop.

"If you tell anyone about this, we will kill you!"

His blood was everywhere and was leaking all over the parquet floor. It was time to leave.

I went home to Sophie. I told her that she was safe, that she was protected, and that my whole crew would now be looking out for her safety now...not just me. It was all over.

What I didn't know at the time was that, sadly, Sophie had started using. She had allowed herself to get mixed up in a bad crowd. When I found out, I was devastated. How would I protect her?

One night, though, not long after her awful incident, I was woken up in the middle of the night by knocking on my window. It was my friend Palmer.

"Baldur, I've found him!" he whispered.

"Found who?"

"Oskar. The dealer. I've got him here with me!"

There, outside in the light of the moon, stood Oskar, the selfish freak who had first introduced my sister Sophie to the needle. I grabbed him by the shoulder and pulled him inside, slamming him down onto the chair in the living room.

The last piece of the Sophie puzzle was finally in place, and that night, we made very, very sure that neither him nor any other abusive idiot would ever go anywhere near my baby sister again.

16

THE GREEN-EYED MONSTER

In 2001, I was lucky enough to cross paths again with a girl named Julia from my hometown. She was fantastic, funny, and kind, and I fell deeply in love with her. Julia and I moved in together, with her family, in a house in downtown Reykjavík. Living with Julia did me a lot of good. I finally got to see how a normal family functioned, but our relationship was often turbulent because I was constantly wrestling with jealousy and distrust issues. I was completely convinced, from the get-go, that Julia would find someone else and eventually abandon me. It was as if all the pain from my childhood, all the neglect and lack of love, came rushing back every time I looked at her.

Julia's parents, who were really great people, also made it very clear that I wouldn't be welcome in their home unless I had a steady job or went to school, so I enrolled in a general bookkeeping and office management program at a new business school. It was a two-semester course with half-day classes, and I worked in masonry repair during the other half of the day to earn more cash. To my complete surprise, I found that learning came naturally to me. I had never considered myself capable of learning because I had so often been told that "nothing would ever come of me." Could it be that I actually wasn't an idiot? Could it be that I had avenues in life

Ice and Fire

available to me other than crime? I allowed myself to entertain these thoughts for a split second, but they vanished just as quickly as they popped into my mind.

I continued with the same lifestyle and used stimulants at school to help me concentrate.

During my school years, I struggled with behavioral issues because of my unstable, chaotic home life. I had been to ten different schools between the first and tenth grades, mostly due to my violent and rebellious attitude. But, at my new business school, I had a wonderful math teacher who completely changed my perspective. He taught me that understanding math really only required putting it into a context that I could relate to. Something that I cared about. We were studying percentages at the time, and all I thought about was improving my drug business. Finally, I could calculate my profits effortlessly and visualize how percentages related to my business. From then on, I excelled at math and was even asked by the teacher to come and teach some classes.

One Saturday night, I shared my exciting new plans with a friend after partying all night. The surprise on her face was priceless and unforgettable.

"Teaching?! You?" she laughed loudly, blowing out a cloud of weed.

I taught at the school that afternoon, and my lecturer was really pleased with me. I was proud of myself. Despite my being stuffed to the gills with coke from the night before, I did a pretty decent job. From then on, I got nothing but straight A's during my first year, ending up taking a more intensive course in finance and management, which I absolutely loved. I loved the parallels between my illicit activities and my newly found management skills. I was in control. Always ensuring we were in profit. I was climbing the underworld financial ladder, and I felt more confident than ever.

I had to be even more discreet with my shady dealings once I moved in with Julia, though. Her parents finally warmed to me, or at least, I thought they did. They were kind and became like a second family, and after my first year of school, Julia's mother, Joan, helped me secure a part-time accounting job at the airline where she worked. My life seemed to be on the up and was finally taking a more positive turn, but sadly, my relationship with Julia began to deteriorate rapidly.

I became increasingly overwhelmed with jealousy and paranoia, and my crazy insecurities sometimes even led me to leave work in the mornings to go and spy on her. Once, I even parked nearby, snuck into the house silently, and then burst into our bedroom, only to find Julia lying peacefully asleep in our bed. Even then, only one paranoid thought crossed my mind -

I'll catch you next time!

Ice and Fire

It never even occurred to me that maybe I was wrong and she was innocent. Why wouldn't she betray me just like everyone else had? How could she possibly love someone like me enough to stay? I was convinced it was only a matter of time before she left me, and the fear of abandonment consumed me day and night and tore our relationship apart. Our arguments became more intense, and we fought relentlessly. Sometimes, I got so angry that I had to run out of the house just to release some of the pent-up tension and fury. I point blank refused to become like those evil, abusive characters from my past, especially my mother's lowlife boyfriends.

My work at the airline was going well, but then Julia and I started to break up and get back together on an almost weekly basis, and eventually, something had to give.

Jealousy and insecurity had torn our love apart, and we ended our relationship.

I was alone again.

17

YOU HAVE BEEN WARNED

One morning, at the age of 23, in April of 2002, I got a phone call that would change everything as I knew it. It was a police detective from Reykjavik.

He asked me to come in for questioning.

"What for?" I asked, knowing full well I had just been involved in a fight downtown a few nights before.

"It's about a young man who's suffered a skull fracture," the detective explained. "There's someone here who claims they saw you headbutting him and knocking his teeth out. You need to come in and give a statement. It allegedly happened on the night of Sunday, April 7th."

I agreed politely to go to the police station, but my blood ran cold when the officer added that the victim had suffered a severe brain bleed.

I winced. Reality had come knocking... right at my front door.

As I sat across from the police officer, I realized that the fight I'd been in had taken a much more serious turn than I had realized. I'd never ever meant for it to end this badly and I was in total shock.

Ice and Fire

I made a decision in my mind right there and then: I needed to stop my crazy party lifestyle, stop drinking and stop hanging around downtown. It was getting out of hand.

I snapped out of my thoughts when the cop mentioned that one of the victims had been brutally kicked repeatedly while totally defenseless, down on the ground.

"Well, I have no clue what you're talking about; I wasn't anywhere near there that night." I insisted.

"Then what's that cut on your forehead from?" the officer asked skeptically, pointing at my head.

"I whacked my head on a kitchen cupboard." I lied.

I was lucky they didn't examine me more closely... I still had a fragment of the guy's front tooth stuck in my forehead wound.

I kept steady in my resistance.

"Are you absolutely sure about this, Baldur?" the cop pressed, leaning into me, obviously still not believing a word I was saying.

"Yeah man, I'm pretty positive!" I replied insolently.

After the interview, I decided to pay a visit to the guy who had gone to the police. His name was Bjorn. I wasn't about to let the guy get away with this nonsense, ratting us out like a chicken. After all, he and his friends had been kicking a man while he was down. I was going to make him understand that he needed to drop the charges. But before I even got to his place, I got a phone call from a notorious underworld figure, warning me to leave Bjorn alone.

"Is he going to drop the charges?" I asked.

"No, he's not," the man replied.

"Well, then you tell him I'm going to have to come over and finish him off!"

Fuming, I headed straight to Bjorn's place, pinned him up against the wall, and punched him one last time flat in the face. I warned him that if he didn't drop the charges immediately, others would be coming after him too. He slid to the ground, defeated, and I left quickly before anybody could see me.

I remained strong and resolute in my decision to stay away from the downtown scene and quit drinking. I kept my promise to myself - no more booze. I was determined to avoid getting into any more over-the-top messes like that again!

My partying days continued, though, as my graduation from business school approached. Every weekend somehow always turned into a party at the apartment, and I invariably ended each night with a bump of coke to counteract the dreamy high of the ecstasy. Then, on weekdays, I'd get all hopped up on methamphetamine and finish my schoolwork. I discovered that stimulants, like meth, helped me concentrate. Most likely because I have ADHD, they allowed me to sit still and actually finish assignments, which I could never ever do without them. I've often wondered how my youth might have played out differently if I had been diagnosed and received proper treatment for my condition.

In early May, with the spring sun shining brightly, I finished work around noon and started reflecting on my accomplishments and success—I was on the verge of graduating, I had been employed by Icelandair for an entire year, and my relationship with Julia had improved. It seemed like we might actually get back together and make it work. But, as always, rather than focusing on these positive aspects, my mind drifted towards a more negative self-loathing thought - something bad must be about to happen. It just wasn't possible for things to go so well for me! The echoes of my past, again, casting shadows on my present.

That was when I received a call from Lara, my aunt and the mother of my close cousin, Aaron, whom I had lost to the ocean at such a young age.

"Baldur, honey, I dreamt about you last night."

She had my attention.

"It was just so vivid. You were walking downtown, our darling Aaron was there with us, and we were following behind you closely.

Baldur…he was absolutely terrified for you! He said to me, 'Mom, please! You need to tell Baldur that he needs to stop this! All of it! Everything! Now!"

She paused and took in a long, deep breath. "Baldur, honey. The voice in my dream told me that you must not go downtown!"

"It's ok, Lara, I've stopped doing all that," I said.

"No, listen! You need to put an end to all of this," she implored me. "The voice in my dream said so! It was our Aaron."

"I know. I'm ready. I've totally given all of that up," I replied.

Even as I said it, I knew I wasn't quite ready to quit everything for good. I may not have given up my drug habit, but I was done hanging around downtown; that much was crystal clear to me. At the same time, though, her dream made me sit up and really think because it came at a time when I was having nightmares. Bad ones.

Every night, I had the same dream. A looming black figure would open my bedroom door and creep slowly and menacingly toward the head of my bed. I always felt awake, but I was totally unable to move, paralyzed by fear. It was as if I was trapped somewhere between sleeping and waking. As soon as this dark being reached me, it would grab me by the throat, and I would simply lie there, frozen in utter terror.

Ice and Fire

It was the worst thing I could imagine – being so completely powerless and defenseless. It was so bad that I started sleeping at the very edge of the bed, and if the nightmare began, I would try to make myself fall out of bed to wake myself up. Someone, or something, seemed to be trying to warn me, not just in Lara's dream but in my own.

Retrospect.

I should have heeded the warning because not long afterward, real tragedy struck.

My phone rang late on a Friday night. My friend, Gary, who was always mischievous, very impulsive, and up for a party, had rung up to persuade me to go downtown with him.

"Ah, come on, man," he insisted, "it's gonna be an awesome night. I'll swing by your place first."

After some laughter and persuasion, I eventually gave in. We sucked down a few beers, snorted a few lines and went bar hopping in downtown Reykjavik. It was a night just like many others, full of all the usual fun and chaos, and it was well into the morning when we decided to stop by a nightclub called Spotlight. The place was closed, but we decided to wait outside for the bouncer to let us in.

It was outside this nightclub on this fateful night that Gary and I got into an altercation with a young man, which ended in the most terrible tragedy.

Something that can never, ever be undone.

At the time, we had no idea how badly he had been injured until the club's bouncer approached me inside, looking very stressed.

"Baldur, the guy's seriously hurt, man. It's bad. You need to turn yourself in!"

My stomach churned with sick anxiety.

"What do you mean seriously hurt? Are you sure?"

I freaked out, panicked and left the party in a stressed rush, knowing the police were probably already looking for me. I managed to get a ride to Stan's place. He had clearly just woken up when he answered the door.

I stammered, delirious and having a hard time breathing. "Stan! I ...I might be responsible for someone's death..."

"Baldur, come on man... relax! We always think that! Come inside." Stan tried to calm me down.

"No. This time, it's different! I think he's going to die!"

"Breathe, my friend. You know it often looks that way when it's not."

I fervently prayed that Stan was right, and still shaking, I sat and smoked a blunt with him, but even the hash high couldn't calm my all-consuming fear and anxiety.

When I couldn't talk anymore, I left Stan and stopped by my friend Palmer's place. He had locked his keys in his car, again and with no idea about my situation, had asked me to help because I knew how to unlock cars using a coat hanger. As I bent the hanger into a makeshift lock pick, I stopped, looked him in the eye, and said,

"I think I may have just killed someone." "What? What do you mean?!" Palmar gasped.

"I got into a fight with a guy downtown. It's bad… I think the guy is really seriously hurt."

"Does anyone know it was you?" "Yes." I started to tear up, "Everyone." I breathed out shakily.

"I have to turn myself in."

Palmer looked at me with concerned affection. I unlocked the car, we hugged each other, and I left.

I lay awake all night in a state of complete shock, and when reality came knocking the next morning, it knocked me right off my feet. The police were indeed looking for me, and the young guy that Gary and I had beaten was still in the hospital and in very bad shape.

I broke down, somehow drove to my uncle's house, and ended up sobbing desperately in his arms.

"I've done so much worse in the past," I cried. "Why? Why him? Why now? Why like this?"

Desperate thoughts and unanswered questions swirled around my head, and it wasn't until much later that day that I managed to pull myself together, stop crying and gather enough strength to ask my uncle Harold to drive me to the police station in Keflavik, so that I could turn myself in.

When I entered, there was nobody at the reception desk, so I had to call out to get the attention of the officer on duty.

"Hi, what can I do for you?" he asked, preoccupied. "I'm turning myself in!" I blurted out.

"What for?"

"Assault and battery."

"Okay. It's a little late for today. Can you come back on Monday?"

What! His response took me totally off guard. I knew the police in Reykjavík were searching for me across the entire city.

"But…I'm wanted."

It took what felt like an age for the officer to grasp the situation. I stood there trembling.

"Oh! Right!" he realized, "Hold on a moment, please."

Finally, the officer got onto the phone with his colleagues in the city, and after a few moments of quiet, his expression changed dramatically.

Within seconds, two officers ran in and arrested me, propped me up against the wall, and cuffed my hands tightly behind my back.

They pushed me around and handled me like a dangerous criminal, putting me into a holding cell before driving me out to the city. In Reykjavík, I was brought immediately before a judge, who sentenced me to eleven days in custody before being transferred to maximum security, where I was placed in solitary confinement.

As the cell door closed, Lara's words echoed through my mind.

"The voice in my dream told me that you must not go downtown, Baldur."

The warning from beyond could not have been clearer.

It was all a very bad dream.

18
JUDGMENT DAY

I looked around my prison cell.

It was tiny, with walls stained a filthy yellow from years of cigarette smoke. There was a toilet at the end of my bed and a hatch in the door for food to be passed to me. I was given a red jumpsuit marked with the name of the prison. I was literally branded.

My first day in solitary confinement felt like an absolute eternity. When I wasn't doing calisthenics to pass the time, I just sat staring up at the ceiling for hours with empty eyes. I was allowed outside into a small roofless pen for an hour each day, though, so I could at least see the sky for a while.

After a few days, I decided to ask my lawyer to bring me my Bible, and I began to pray. I prayed and I prayed, with all the might I could muster, that the boy I'd beaten would survive. But as much as I prayed, the harrowing guilt still consumed me. If only I had listened to my intuition and made better choices that night. If only I hadn't gone to the Spotlight nightclub. If only I had paid attention to what my aunt Lara had told me.

If only…

On Saturday afternoon the following week, after days of hoping and praying, a prison guard finally handed me a phone through the hatch in my cell door.

"Hello, Baldur."

"Hello!" I whispered.

I could hear by the tone of my lawyer's voice that he didn't have the good news I'd been hoping for.

"I'm sorry to say that the case has taken a turn for the worse, Baldur. I'm afraid the boy died today."

I gasped and shoved the phone back through the hatch as if it were on fire. Then, I just sat there, motionless, not breathing, enveloped in a profound and infinite darkness. When I heard the hatch on the cell door slam shut, I felt as if the door to my future had been locked once and for all. It was all over.

I somehow survived through the days that followed, and a few days later, the guards told me that I was going to be transferred to 'General Population.' This meant I would be moving into the prison itself and into a cell block with ten other inmates. Although it was still a prison, it felt like freedom compared to the deafening silence and crushing feelings of shame I had endured in isolation. As I was getting dressed to leave, the guards handed me back my things and the wad of cash that I had on me when I was arrested. They warned me to hide the money and gave me their tips for 'Gen Pop' survival. Their speech sent me straight into self-defense mode, and I walked over to my new cell block with clenched fists and an impenetrable invisible wall around me. I felt like I was being transported into a lion's den, where I'd have to fight for my survival.

Once I got to know the other inmates, though, I realized they were just ordinary guys like me. But I also realized it was important not to reveal any weaknesses, just as I had learned from the Reykjavík drug trade. As a child drifting between relatives' homes, I'd developed a real talent for reading my surroundings - I'd honed it to a fine art.

It wasn't long before I was attacked for the first time, though. While playing soccer in the gym, I rubbed it in the other team's face that we were winning. Let's just say it didn't go down too well. As I backed away from one of the guys who was taunting me, I felt someone approach me from behind, grab me tightly around the waist, and lift me up. I reacted quickly, turning around, slamming him to the ground and grabbing him by the neck. By the time the guards arrived, it was all over. The guy left the gym, and my team went back, shooting goals. I knew that I was going to be in this place for a long time, and I had to show them what I was made of. I couldn't let the others think I'd ever give in to anyone.

After that incident, I was assigned to share a corridor with a car salesman named Tommy, who had received a 12-year sentence. The

Ice and Fire

longest drug-related sentence ever given in Iceland. Tommy was on top of the prison drug dealing game, and we quickly formed an easy and profitable partnership. I knew as soon as I arrived there that I was going to have to get sober, but I could easily pick up some extra cash by selling dope inside. I would procure the drugs, and he would handle the sales, with the profits divided between us.

The drugs were smuggled into the prison, concealed inside of the mules who carried them. When I say 'inside,' I mean it was concealed up their backsides. So, early on, when a shipment's packaging broke, contaminating the product with fecal matter and a horrendous odor, our sales plummeted. Basically, it reeked of feces. I voiced my concerns, but crazy Tommy, as always, stayed optimistic and suggested that we simply lower the price.

"Nobody's going to buy this disgusting stuff," I laughed.

"Oh, please! I can sell it in no time!" he replied with a smirk.

It didn't take long for Tommy to turn a hefty profit from the foul-smelling speed. He sold it mostly to intravenous drug users in the prison who didn't notice the odor. Our unconventional method of smuggling wasn't limited to drugs. Tommy even managed once to sneak a cell phone into prison, a massive old Nokia 5110 with an oversized battery.

"How on earth did you fit that thing up there?" I asked, struggling not to laugh.

"I just sat on it," he deadpanned, sending me into fits of hysterical laughter.

"Too bad it was right before my appointment with the chiropractor." "What !?" I couldn't stop laughing.

"During the appointment, as he was twisting me to adjust my back, the damn phone pressed on my bladder, and I pissed myself." he cracked up.

We roared with laughter; the situation could not have been much more absurd.

Despite the initial discomfort of "carrying" the phone in this way, it was a fantastic stroke of luck. The regular phones in the prison were always monitored, but not our gigantic Nokia, which made it much easier to bring our product inside the prison walls. Sadly, many years later, after his time in prison, Tommy died by accident. The drug squad caught him with a huge quantity of pure cocaine on him. He swallowed it all at once, but the packaging it was wrapped in burst inside him and killed him.

Later on, I formed a new partnership with a guy named Karl, who had been arrested in one of Iceland's largest-ever drug busts. We clicked immediately, he started supplying me with products to sell, and we divvied the profits. We were practically swimming in the stuff, and unfortunately, I had also started using it again myself. We used Ritalin and Speed for bartering with fellow inmates, but this did not sit at all well with the head Prison Warden, Cole, who was dealing daily with a suddenly rampant drug problem. Nearly all the inmates were failing their urine drug tests, so we had to be really sly and devious with our in-house dealings.

Eighteen months later, in early 2003, I found myself being transported to the Supreme Court to face five judges. Whenever I was brought into a courtroom, I always took my Bible with me. It somehow gave me some kind of reassurance and faith that I could put all of this behind me. On the way there, I sat in a small cage at the back of a Land Cruiser, with guards up front, all separated by bars. I opened my Bible and turned to the Book of Job: the man who had lost everything. It resonated deeply with me. I wasn't expecting good news from the Supreme Court and was bracing myself for a heavy sentence, but I had no idea just how heavy it would be. My family and friends had all shown up to offer me support in the courtroom. The judge instructed me to stand. I stood and prepared myself for the worst.

"The accused, Baldur Freyr Einarsson, is hereby sentenced to six years in prison, with time served from May 26, 2002,"

He continued on, but I couldn't hear a word.

The sentencing painted me as a ruthless, violent offender with no mitigating circumstances.

I was totally and utterly crushed.

Gary's sentence was increased from two years to three, as he had tried to shift the blame onto me in the lead-up to the verdict. I hated him for it. The medical examiner who performed the autopsy supported my claim that I had inflicted very few blows, emphasizing that it was Gary's final kick that caused the victim to fall and hit his head, ultimately killing him.

I stood frozen, profoundly disappointed in my lawyer. My mom came over to comfort me and asked if I wanted to speak with him.

"What would I even have to say to him?" I shouted, throwing my Bible down in exhausted frustration. It seemed to me that God had obviously completely forsaken me, and I couldn't imagine how things could possibly get any worse. It was that very same day that I heard about what happened to Tommy after his release from prison. My freedom had been ripped away from me, but at least I was still alive.

19

INSIDE

As time wore on inside, Cole, our determined and very agitated Warden, became increasingly consumed with rage at the rampant drug situation. The sudden and very obvious surge in drug activity within his prison walls completely confounded him. In a desperate attempt to stop it, he organized for Karl, my dealing partner and a well-known notorious troublemaker, to be moved away from me to a prison up in the north of Iceland. It was nothing more than a tactical move in his game, but it only annoyed me more.

So, I decided to switch things up a bit to suit my game and get an inmate named Larry to switch corridors with a new guy called John, who I'd heard would be an asset. Warden Cole obviously caught wind of my plans, summoned me to his office, and completely lost his cool.

"Baldur, I'm the one in charge of this prison, not you!" he bellowed, pounding his desk repeatedly. "I decide who goes where, not you!"

I kept a straight face but laughed to myself.

"I'm not sure what you're talking about, Cole," I replied politely.

"You know damn well what I mean, Baldur, and I'll make sure you don't forget it!" he threatened furiously.

After this bizarre encounter, I marched, sniggering, straight back to my corridor and approached Larry. "Mate, you're moving to 2B. I know the guys there will make you feel right at home."

He agreed and immediately put in a transfer request, and the angry warden, oblivious to my influence, approved it. As soon as Larry left his cell, I spread the word: If anyone other than John tried to join our corridor, they would regret it.

After weeks of this standoff, I thoroughly enjoyed watching Cole eat his own words and finally transfer John to the now-vacant cell on the third floor.

The guards were also generally very vindictive and power-hungry, and in later years, I made my opinions on treatment during my "correctional stay" at the prison very clear publicly. They could be inhumane and plain malicious at times. One time, I gave one of the duty officers his comeuppance by pursuing his niece. I asked her to be my girlfriend just to irritate him. When she came to visit me, the guards made sure we could only see one another with glass between us to prevent any intimate contact.

"I'm going to get her pregnant," I told the boys. "Then I'll be part of his family, and he'll never get rid of me."

Ice and Fire

Laughter filled the room.

Our relationship continued, and when the prison started to block my efforts to see her, I even took my story to the papers.

"The prison is abusing their rights and preventing me from seeing my girlfriend..."

To be honest, the visitors' wing could be a very interesting place, with, oftentimes, sounds of pleasure so loud and intense that it made any conversation with visitors hilariously nearly impossible.

This was my daily life inside. As far as I was concerned, it was a full out war between us and Cole and the guards. I felt increasingly confident, and my efforts to get drugs in any way and I started to become more daring. One day, I booked an appointment with a doctor in town for my eczema. I made the trip under close supervision, but the night before, I'd arranged for one of my contacts on the outside to discreetly stash 150 carefully wrapped ecstasy tablets in the doctor's bathroom trash bin. We had smuggled in so much molly that the prison was practically turned on its head, and now we needed more.

When I arrived, I excused myself to the restroom, where the pills had supposedly been hidden an hour earlier. I turned the trash can upside down and emptied its contents onto the floor.

Nothing.

Shaking with anxiety, I left and snuck into the adjacent restroom, my hope dwindling with each passing second. What had the dealer done? With my stress and frustration mounting, I went back into the doctor's office and finished my appointment, determined to call the dealer the second I left and unravel the mystery of the vanishing ecstasy.

When I got back to the prison, I was subjected to another thorough and uncomfortable search by the guards. They were meticulous and left no stone unturned, scouring every possible hiding spot, but they found nothing. It was clear - the dealer had left me high and dry.

Still suspicious, Warden Cole made his way to my cell, a sardonic grin on his already menacing face –

"Get your shoes on; you're being sent for a more comprehensive search at the medical clinic."

Any lingering frustration about the missing pills was gone. Whatever "comprehensive search" the warden had had in store for me would be fruitless. Relief washed over me - I had been way too careless, but I was going to be fine.

Arriving at the clinic, I was made to lie down as a doctor performed an extremely invasive procedure, shoving a camera up my rectum.

Afterward, I overheard the doctor's conversation on the phone. "He's as clean as a whistle," he informed my buddy, the warden. I could almost feel the rage on the other end of the line.

Upon my return to the prison, the guards immediately confined me to a cell dedicated to body searches. Something fishy was definitely going on.

After a short wait, a string of guards entered the cell for what they called a 'security search.'

"What's a security search?"

I'd never heard the term in all my time there and started to feel uneasy about the presence of so many guards.

"Stand with your legs apart and your arms in the air!" said Thomas, who just so happened to be the warden's brother.

I hesitantly assumed the position.

The guards lined up around me, ready to grab hold of my arms and legs. I was completely bewildered and had no clue what was going to happen next. All of a sudden, Thomas started frisking my entire body. Once he'd thoroughly groped me, up and down, he crouched to pat down my legs, looked me straight in the eye, and grabbed my crotch.

"Well, aren't you hung like a horse," he said in a sardonic voice.

Then, I realized why the guards were standing so close to my arms and legs. They thought I'd go ape and lose my temper so they could throw me into solitary.

"You're a disgusting pervert!" I shouted at him. "How dare you touch me up like that!"

I looked at the guards around me.

"You are all witnesses!"

They looked down and remained silent. The atmosphere was charged. I looked at Thomas, using all of my strength not to just knee him in his face.

"Are you done?"

Uncomfortable, the guards left the cell one by one.

"Thomas, you do realize this is sexual assault, don't you? I'm going to press charges."

He paused, turned around, and left without responding.

I immediately booked an appointment with the prison psychiatrist and shared my story with him before reporting Thomas to the police.

Of course, I knew sexual harassment wasn't their game; they only wanted to degrade me into losing my temper and attacking them. But I decided to seize this unexpected and devious shift in their tactics as an opportunity to turn the tables on them.

To give them a taste of their own bitter medicine.

20

GRADUATION DAY

As the days turn into weeks and weeks into months, one way or another, you somehow just find a way to adapt to your circumstances. Life inside was rough, but it also did have its moments. There was one guard I grew to respect and trust; his name was Jonathan. He supervised those of us tasked with outdoor labor, a duty the guards playfully called 'The Gulag.'

It was as monotonous as it was pointless. We'd dig a hole or a shallow trench, arranging the landscaping rocks to the left and the soil we'd dug up to the right. Once the task was complete, we'd fill the hole with the same rocks and bury the entire thing with the soil. Being outside, even with the futility of our tasks, offered a welcome escape from the monotony of prison life. I willingly took part in 'The Gulag' only because it spared me from the sluggish snail's pace of time inside the prison walls.

One sunny day, as I strolled into the work shed on my coffee break to relax in the chair I had always sat on (and actually even painted gold, as a joke), I found it already occupied by someone I hadn't seen before. A newcomer. I was annoyed, and without a second thought, I told him to get out of my chair.

"No!" he shot back, rudely.

His response stunned me.

"Get out of my seat now, you moron!" I seethed.

"No." he grinned. "New people, new rules. Get over it!"

In the blink of an eye, I lunged at the idiot and threw him from the chair, slamming him into the wall and leaving him sprawled on the ground. By the look on his face, I think he had a full understanding of the fact that he was in no position to be laying down any new rules in this place.

In the middle of the fight, I noticed that Jonathan, the new guard, had quietly left the shed and was nowhere to be seen. Stressed out, I assumed he had gone to call more guards and braced myself for a 24-hour stint in solitary. After a minute, I heard footsteps approach. The shed door swung open, and to my surprise, it was Jonathan standing alone.

"Well? Shouldn't we get back to work, guys?" he calmly asked, easing the tangible tension in the room.

I was completely baffled. Why hadn't Jonathan thrown me into solitary? I knew full well that this could potentially land him in deep trouble. My face was just one big question mark as I left the shed, but that day marked the beginning of my trust in him. I guess they weren't all bad.

From then on, we began chatting regularly, and I felt an interesting connection with him that would only get closer later on.

We spent hours talking about everything under the sun. Sometimes, he'd broach the topic of God and Jesus, and I'd tease him, all in good fun. I'd given up on all of that. After all, what good had it done me?

Jonathan's time with us was relatively short, but he made my prison experience far more bearable, even though the warden and a lot of the guards were still constantly out to get me.

Another source of solace for me during this time was my younger sister, Hanna. We were always there for each other. When she was just a child, maybe around seven years old, she had to write a poem for a school project, and I'd helped her with it. She always remembered it, and during my time behind bars, she went the extra mile to make me feel good by filming a video of herself reciting the poem just for me. It was so sweet, and it moved me deeply. Such a genuine, heartfelt, and loving gesture from a beautiful person.

Throughout my incarceration, I kept my studies going and eventually graduated from a university course, which was a huge achievement for someone in my family. On my graduation day, we held a party with my buddies, my family, and some of my old church friends. It was a stunningly beautiful sunny day, and Hanna surprised me with a fantastic cake decorated with a marzipan picture of the cartoon character, 'Johnny Bravo' (Hanna had always thought he resembled me), standing behind bars in a prison uniform. I loved how she simply accepted me for who I was and was always able to lighten things up and make us all laugh. Sophie, my other sister, had, by this time, stepped into my role as the caregiver for our younger brother, Daniel, and had even named her first son after me – such an honor. A while later, we held his baptism in the prison's solitary confinement wing (despite repeated refusals from the prison admin) because she'd insisted that she wanted me to hold the baby for this special moment. My siblings' unconditional love and support kept me going and, most of all, kept me sane.

During my final months in prison, I carried on dealing drugs and clashing with the warden, who shuffled me between different floors and cells in a useless attempt to "maintain discipline and order." Whenever the time came for my daytime leaves, I would avoid any substances that could be detected with drug tests and use Ritalin, opioids, and acid to keep up my facade. Just before I left, I applied for transitional housing and found out that I would be obligated to work full-time to stay there. I also made the decision to enroll in law school at the University of Iceland and keep studying.

As a start, a friend of mine, who owned a tanning salon downtown, agreed to "employ" me and give me an office where I could manage my work.

On my last night in prison, I slept surprisingly soundly, very relieved that I would finally be rid of the Warden and his annoying minions. I couldn't wait for the freedom. The halfway house where I'd be staying had far fewer rules. I'd only have to be home for dinner and stay in the house during weekend evenings. On weekdays, I'd need to be indoors by 11 pm and couldn't leave until 7 am the following morning. This suited me just fine; anything was better than where I'd been.

The next day, I packed up my stuff and loaded my bag into the back of the prison's Land Cruiser, which had transported me to and from the prison countless times. A feeling of unbelievable elation that words cannot possibly describe filled me as we drove out of that gate, away from that suffocating world.

This time, I wouldn't be coming back.

21

HALFWAY HOUSE

I was finally out, but during my eight months in rehabilitation housing, I pretty much immediately fell straight back into my old bad habits. I started using it again, and harder than ever.

I'd also figured out a sure-fire method for cheating on the regular urine tests. It's amazing the lengths people will go to when something tries to come between a user and their high. Just before each test, I'd tuck a small bottle filled with clean urine discreetly between my buttocks. The bottle had a tiny tube that I'd place under my penis before putting on my underwear. Like magic, with a quick clench of my cheeks, I'd discreetly transfer the clean urine through the tube and into the test cup, which I would then hand over with a smile.

After a few weeks, I rented a small basement apartment and dove headfirst back into my business dealings. I'd made even more connections while I was inside, and I even started to dabble in importing drugs from abroad. I started dealing in massive quantities of drugs wholesale with a network of guys, and the money started streaming in rapidly, making it blatantly obvious to anyone who wanted to take a closer look that I was more than just a struggling student working part-time at a tanning salon.

As months passed, unsurprisingly, the narcotics officers started catching on. One afternoon, I went to Palmer's apartment, only to bump into two very uptight-looking men in the stairwell. They blocked my way, pulled out their badges, and waved them in my face-

"Narcotics division!"

At that very moment, I had 50 grams of cocaine in my underwear. "Time for a pat down!"

"Sure guys, no problem," I said nonchalantly, but actually crapping myself.

I began by casually removing my jacket and then undid my pants right there in the stairwell. I knew that the only way to avoid landing back in a cell was to act as if I had absolutely nothing to hide. I stood there with my trousers around my ankles, feigning indifference, and ready to remove my underwear, when suddenly one of the officers stopped me.

They carried on their search, inspecting the pockets of my trousers and jacket as I watched on, praying that they wouldn't notice the unusual bulges in my underwear. Despite finding nothing, they arrested me and put me in a cell in an old police station just outside of the city. They deliberately kept me there too long so that I'd be late to the halfway house.

Ice and Fire

I just sat there, underpants full of cocaine, completely astounded by the fact that they hadn't discovered my secret. Pulling a fast one on the drug squad seemed like child's play compared to selling drugs in prison - these guys were easy.

Around the same time, I got back into a partnership, dealing with my old friend from the inside, Karl. We really connected again, and in a strange turn of events, which I could never have imagined, I ended up working in another black-market industry.

Karl and I opened a brothel.

Karl was living partly in Brazil at the time and started convincing Brazilian women he'd met to come to Iceland and work for us. They could earn more than double working in Reykjavik than in their home country. I was all in. We got the location sorted out, got the girls in, and it was all go.

While running the brothel, we partied hard, and despite being constantly high and neck deep in drugs, I always managed to stay mostly on top of things and maintain a mask of sobriety. Very few people knew the truth about my real problems. The business moved slowly initially, and I started to think that maybe the prostitution racket wouldn't be as profitable as we had hoped. After all, most of our clients were friends and acquaintances, and it just wasn't proving to be lucrative enough. So, one day, on a whim, I decided to place an ad in the personal columns of a website related to 'Adult

Services.' Sure as daylight it worked, and demand surged to the point where we needed a full-time receptionist to manage our bookings. What I found the craziest was that our busiest hours were always during the day, especially around midday, and that many of our customers were family men. The ladies were kept very busy, and our new business was blossoming.

The staff at the halfway house often grew suspicious and tried to bust me with urine tests, but nothing ever came of it; I passed them all. I'd even gone so far as to sneak my girlfriend into my room overnight and climb out the window the next morning before I left. The only rules I respected were the ones I made myself.

I had it all under control. Or so I thought.

One crazy morning in 2006, I was hanging out in my basement hideaway after a heavy night of partying. I called a friend who'd been holding onto some LSD for me and asked him to bring it over. It was meticulously wrapped, with the papers tightly packed together. I tore it open as soon as it arrived, grabbed six and threw them straight into my mouth. I did notice that the LSD sheets felt a bit thick, but as I was already in an altered state, I didn't realize that each one I'd taken was actually several papers stacked on top of each other.

I swallowed them before I could even second-guess myself, and I had taken a lot. I'd, of course, experienced bad trips before, but this time, I got so high, so fast, that I didn't even realize it until I called 911. I barely managed to breathe into the phone before they hung up on me. I was a goner. The next thing I knew, I found myself standing in front of a wall of wooden cabinets, completely hypnotized and feeling trapped. I found an iron door in the room and started pounding on it, over and over repeatedly. I tried to ask for help, but I couldn't form a sentence, and my speech was completely garbled, terrifying my girlfriend and other people at the house.

When the police finally arrived, I was in another world - in the midst of a complete psychotic breakdown. It took a few police officers several attempts to restrain me and fasten me to a gurney. They rushed me into the ER, and I was given an injection of some sort to calm me down.

Emergency medical report, March 4, 2006.

Baldur is a healthy 27-year-old male who arrived at the emergency room accompanied by several police officers. An ambulance was called to Baldur's home. He was extremely agitated, and according to his girlfriend, he had been using large quantities of drugs in the past 48 hours. Ecstasy tablets, speed, LSD, hash, cocaine and more.

Diagnosis: Poisoning by unspecified drugs, medicaments, and biological substances. T50.9

Apparently, I was at the hospital for several hours, but when I came to, I found myself standing in the middle of a cell with absolutely no recollection of how I had ended up there or what had happened. I was more disoriented and confused than I had ever been in my entire life, and it frightened me.

I looked down at my hands and saw that my knuckles were covered in blood.

I was terrified. What had I done?

Dazed and stressed beyond belief, I rang the bell inside the cell and tried to talk into the speaker. "Please…please, can you tell me what happened to me?" "You don't remember?" a cop finally answered

"No! Did I hurt anyone?" I asked with a lump in my throat, verging on tears.

"Only a couple of cops."

It was a living nightmare. I stood shaking, waiting for what felt like an eternity for anyone to come back and tell me what to do. Finally, the prison director appeared.

"Baldur, you're not being charged, but there's some bad news. The drug test you took revealed everything you've been taking."

I knew what that meant - straight to prison.

Ice and Fire

27 years old and there I was, back in a cell and back in limbo. The cops refused to tell me when I would be released, but I had managed to last six months in the transitional housing, which meant I only had two months left until I completed two-thirds of my sentence. Some officials contacted me and came all the way up to the prison to show me some papers that they wanted me to sign. They were parole papers.

The woman in charge asked, "Why is it, Baldur, that your tests were positive for every drug imaginable?"

"Um...I slipped up a little."

"Yes, I see that. You've been providing clean samples for months, and then, all of a sudden, all of this shows up in your system. Strange..."

"I can't explain it, sorry."

She handed me the paper, looking me in the eye. "We've requested that you be placed on probation for drugs and alcohol for one year."

"Seriously? Isn't that just for winos?" I asked, annoyed.

"Considering your test results, we won't be releasing you without supervision."

"Are you kidding me? I don't have a drug problem!"

"It's simple, Baldur, you're only going out on parole if you meet these conditions."

"Great, where do I sign?" I snapped back.

I left the meeting feeling attacked and annoyed. Why on earth was I subject to conditions that usually only applied to inmates who were hardcore alcoholics? I was hugely irritated, but at the same time, I was reassured by the fact that I at least had an out.

When I walked out of the prison, it was a bright sunny day and to my total delight, there was a limo waiting for me. My friends had all come to pick me up in style and had planned a massive party and an impromptu trip to Amsterdam. I looked up at the sky, put on my sunglasses, hugged my friends, and rolled a joint. Making a grand show-off exit was my way of flipping the finger to these people one last time. A final gesture of defiance.

Although I never showed it, it took me a while to regain my strength after my stint in intensive care, and I was very well aware that I needed to make big changes in my life. I was still treading on dangerously thin ice, and being on parole, I wasn't truly free. One of the many advantages of no longer being constantly monitored, though, was that I could party without the fear of police bothering me. At our parties, tables were openly covered with plates piled sky high with all of the drugs you could possibly imagine, and our latest game was to snort a line without knowing what it was and then wait for its effects to sweep us into euphoria. I was on cloud nine, and I was determined not to let probation hold me back.

I was free, alive, and I made it my mission to spread positivity and make sure that everyone had a fantastic time at my parties. I was Dr Feelgood. Sex, drugs… and more sex and drugs. Gone were the curfews and early morning returns that had confined me to the halfway house.

Laughter, lust, highs, and happiness filled the air as I made up for all the joy I had missed during my years of incarceration. I wasn't a kid anymore, but when the party finally came to an end, I just headed somewhere else and simply moved on to my next adventure, night after night after night.

Then, in what started to feel like a curse, I had another strange, vivid dream. Only, this time there was no dark figure looming. I saw four angels in front of me. They picked me up and lifted me up into the clouds, stopping in front of a large clock that seemed to float in the sky. As they held me there, I heard a powerful, compassionate voice resonating around me.

"You're heading in the wrong direction. You must make a change."

"Change? How?" I asked.

"You need to able to look back and be at peace with all that you've done."

"What if I can't?"

My gaze was abruptly pulled back to the clock. I was mesmerized, and I watched on as the second hand began to tick loudly.

Tick… tick… tick…

I gasped and couldn't catch my breath - it was as if I was having the air sucked out of me and was slowly suffocating, and yet, I felt a strange sense of peace and protection from the beings holding me up. I started to give in, to surrender, and just as I was about to lose consciousness to the bliss of suffocation, the second hand stopped ticking - and I woke up with a fright.

I sat up, shaking and sweating. I was exhausted. It was time. I knew I needed to change, but I just couldn't see how. I was in way too deep.

Something was going to have to give.

The clock was ticking.

22

ON MY KNEES

In January of 2007, something happened to me.

A sudden, inexplicable feeling of flat-out fear gripped me. Worried, I initially blamed it on my drug use, so I began to try to monitor and control my drug intake, but nothing changed, and the fear persisted, especially when I was alone.

It started to plague my nights and kept me from sleeping. I tossed and turned, and eventually, I even started hearing voices around me and seeing outlines of large, ominous, shadowy figures. I felt trapped. It started to happen so often that I was suddenly scared of being alone because whenever I was alone, they were there.

One evening, in a completely inebriated drug-induced high, these ghostly dark entities even chased me all the way down to the harbor, terrorizing me.

"Just jump into the sea, you monster! Get it over with! Look what you've done to everyone around you!" they breathed.

When I finally came to my senses and woke up, I found myself standing, shivering, on an old pier by the ocean, filled with paranoia. It all felt so real. I was desperate. I should have felt great; business was booming, but nothing that I'd fought for with my blood, sweat, and tears had brought me the happiness that I'd expected.

If anything, I only felt worse.

The anxiety continued every day, and desperate for some kind of relief, I turned to spirituality. I went to a store I'd heard of called 'Better Life' that sold spiritual and self-improvement products. I went in with an open mind and bought every kind of spiritual protection trinket I could find - crystals, calming CDs, energy stones, burning sage - really anything I could lay my hands on to try to clear out and purify my apartment.

By this point, I'd slowed down my drug use a bit. I was doing less coke, used amphetamines to keep myself going in the day, and only smoked weed after 6 pm to bring myself down. Despite this, though, my fear persisted, even though I still couldn't put my finger on exactly what it was that I was afraid of.

One day, after weeks of being tormented beyond belief, I decided to pull myself together and go to a twelve-step meeting.

I walked up the stairs to the meeting hall, my hoodie pulled over my head and slumped onto a couch at the back. The meeting started, and the moderator started singling out individuals and asking them to share. In my completely paranoid state, I was convinced that they were all ganging up on me. I hated these phony people. Why couldn't they just say things to my face instead of thinly veiling their comments in this patronizing, judgmental way? My paranoia and frustration were completely overwhelming. But, for some reason, despite my skepticism and anger, I somehow discovered a small glimmer of hope that day and decided that I would give these meetings another chance.

I chose my sponsor carefully. I knew that I needed someone I could be completely honest with without worrying about facing someone's judgment. I asked a guy named Edward, whom I knew from the old days. I knew he had been sober for some time and was a good guy.

I was in a rush, as always, and insisted on speeding through the twelve steps as fast as I could. I didn't have the time or the patience to take it slowly.

Over time, with Edwards's help, I completed the first three steps of the twelve-step program. I acknowledged that I was an addict, that I had no control over my life, and that no human power could save me from my addictive behavior, and finally, I accepted that God could help me if I turned to him.

My sponsor, Edward, encouraged me to pray -

"Now it's your turn, Baldur! Now we get on our knees."

"What, right now?"

"Yes! Right now!" he said.

I wasn't sure. We knelt together, clasped our hands, and he led me in reciting the prayer, one verse at a time. When we were finished, Edward congratulated me for completing the first three steps, and I was proud of myself for facing these painful tasks head-on.

Also, I had to admit to myself, after all of this time, that it just felt good to pray.

I found myself thinking about how my knees had taken on a new purpose! Edward always emphasized the importance of kneeling in prayer every morning and every night. In the past, I'd mostly used my knees to cause trouble, injure, and mistreat others, but now I was going to use them to humble myself. To heal. I shared this revelation with the group at our next meeting, and it elicited a few laughs.

"I just discovered that knees weren't created to slam into people's faces, but to kneel before God!"

Little by little, as I became more excited about my recovery, I started going to daily noon meetings and sometimes even evening sessions on the same day. Then, as part of the program, I started to write lists of my frustrations and fears. Only one person made his way onto my fear list - myself. Looking back, I now realize how perfectly this illustrates my total lack of self-understanding. The image I'd built up around myself had blinded me to just how terrified

I really was. Terrified of being alone, of being unlovable, of being rejected.

Edward and I went over these lists together, thoroughly discussing and praying over each item. When we had finished, Edward stood up, looked me in the eye and said,

"Do you know what your problem is, Baldur?"

I anxiously waited for his answer, expecting empathy because of my challenging and tragic childhood.

"You!" he replied. "You are your problem,"

Sitting across from him, looking into his eyes, I felt a strong urge to pop him in the jaw. I did not like hearing that, but I knew deep inside that he was right.

I was determined to stay the course, and as I delved deeper into the twelve steps, I came to understand the importance of complete honesty about my shortcomings and flaws. It wasn't easy, but I decided, with the help of my mom and my girlfriend, to write down my flaws to take to my next meeting.

Together, we agreed on three significant flaws

Irritability and moodiness. Never being on time.

Impatience.

However, when I met my sponsor that night, he wasn't at all satisfied with my list. There was a long, uncomfortable silence as he read.

Considerably longer, at least, I thought, than it should have taken to read over three very simple sentences.

"Is this everything?" he finally asked, looking up at me.

"Yup!" I answered, satisfied with myself and proud of my work.

"Aren't you going to mention dishonesty?"

"What? Why? I'm not dishonest!"

"Baldur. You import and sell drugs…"

At first, I resisted, but our discussion carried on late into the night, and it triggered a new thought. I decided to look up and explore the concept of the seven deadly sins -

Lust. Gluttony. Greed. Sloth. Wrath. Pride. Envy

I started filling my notebook to the brim with thoughts and reflections, and somehow, I started to see everything in a new, different light. I started opening up to my weaknesses, getting down on my knees and praying, morning and at night. I learned and recited the twelve-step prayer, asking God to help me remove my character defects and grant me the strength to do better. I could become a better man.

With each step of the twelve-step program, I began to feel more awake and clear. Step 9, which called for making amends for wrongdoings, led me to confront my violent past. I chose to make amends with a man named Steven, a previous boyfriend of my mom's, whom I had violently assaulted years before. I had met him outside the ER as we were both leaving after an incident, and I beat him so badly that he had to turn around and go back inside. My inner struggle with this apology was intense, with every fiber of my being crying out in protest, but I just prayed for strength to go through with it.

Steven agreed to meet me as long as we did so in a busy public place. I understood and suggested a café in Reykjavik.

"I'm here because I want to apologize for beating you up at the hospital."

Steven looked shocked.

"I would like to make it up to you, so if there's anything I can do..."

"No! No!" he interrupted, trying to lie his way out of trouble. "No need. You know I was always so kind to your mom!"

What?! A huge wave of rage threatened to engulf me, and at that moment, I had to grab onto the edge of the table to anchor myself. Did he really just say that? I held my breath. He treated her anything but kindly! Nothing had changed.

Desperate to regain my composure and not send him back to the ER again, I closed my eyes, breathed out, and silently said the 'prayer of resentment' I had learned and came to know so well. It worked, and slowly, I found the strength to give in and acknowledge his words. After all, this wasn't about him; it was about me.

A little while later, I put my pride aside, thanked him and left.

A peculiar feeling came over me as I stepped outside the coffee shop. I felt a new sense of freedom. The struggle to get to this point and the fact that I'd kept a level head and not responded to Steven's comment about my mom made the victory even sweeter. I felt transformed. I had removed the first brick from the great wall that I'd built up around my truth. The impenetrable wall that told me that I was never enough, that I was worthless, that I was, and always would be, always the blackest of the black sheep.

That evening, it just so happened that my cousin Denni invited me to join him at a home fellowship group hosted by one of his friends. They wanted me to share some of my songs with them. I went to the meeting full of energy, and the joyous group of strangers welcomed me. I immediately felt right at home and surprisingly full of hope. They listened to me, supported me, and guided me through a heartfelt prayer, accepting Jesus. And just like that, in that instant, somehow, all of my unease and anxiety flowed out of me and just disappeared. The constant fear that had held me in its relentless iron grip for over a year had simply vanished.

I dropped to my knees and cried, filled with a sense of belonging and purpose. What a night!

Just before we left that evening, Denni's friend announced that she was moving and wouldn't be able to host the next meeting.

"I'm up for it!" I blurted out loudly, without thinking, and then laughed.

In that one spontaneous moment, I made a monumental decision. A life choice that would have far-reaching consequences way beyond my imagination.

My mind buzzed with excitement and ideas. It was very clear to me what I had to do next. I would create a new community. A unique, open-minded, spiritual fellowship group founded on nothing but love. The change I had so long been waiting for was coming, and I knew the second I said it that I was about to embark on an unchartered path of healing, redemption, and service to others.

And I knew the perfect place to do it. The old brothel.

23
SIMPLY THE BEST

I happily stuck to my word, and in 2007, we started our new Christian fellowship group in the old brothel. The comic irony wasn't lost on anyone, and it was amazing! Our meetings were about as far from conventional as you can get and about as rough as they come - we smoked inside, read from the Bible together, partied, and belted out praise songs at the top of our lungs late into the night.

It was wild, exciting, and fun, but soon, it became clear to me that Denni (my cousin) was on the verge of relapsing into drugs and falling off the wagon again. I could see he was really struggling, and not wanting to let him down, I decided to use drastic measures - I refused to let him out of my apartment or out of my sight. He was basically grounded. Of course, this didn't work, and he snuck out at the very next opportunity and sprinted off down the street. Annoyed, I threw on my shoes and bolted out after him, still just in my tank top. I ran after him as if my life depended on it, determined not to lose him to the clutches of addiction again.

I finally managed to catch up to him and jump on him a few blocks away, stopping him in his tracks. I dragged him back up the street, kicking and screaming. He tried to resist, but I was just stronger.

Ice and Fire

"Denni!" I shouted. "You are not going to get high!"

"Let me go, you idiot!" he yelled at me, furious.

I was halfway up the street, holding him, when I noticed a Police car was parked diagonally across it a block away. It suddenly dawned on me what this must have looked like from the point of view of a passerby. A violent ex-con dragging a man forcefully down the street. Not to mention that everyone knew what went on in apartment 23. I quickly released Denni from my grip, scared of the consequences.

Denni ducked from the scene as fast as his legs could carry him, and that night, he went on a massive drug binge, only to return to my place to get sober. I had failed in my attempt to prevent his relapse, and I felt terrible for him.

My cousin's descent back into addiction was a clear reminder to me of just how difficult it was to break free from the grip of drug dependence. Something big had changed in me, yes, and I was still wholeheartedly living by the twelve steps, but at the same time, I was still doing things that were simply wrong. My morality and thought patterns still needed substantial change. It was not lost on me that I was still involved in the illegal drug business, importing and selling drugs, despite my newfound faith.

On the plus side, our new fellowship at the old brothel continued to expand rapidly, and we started noticing that even traditional

Christians were sneaking into our meetings, their coughs giving them away amidst the cloud of cigarette smoke that hung in the air. We soon decided that maybe it wasn't the best idea to smoke inside and took breaks between preaching sessions to go outside.

To my surprise, even my dad, who was living at a nearby home for disabled people, began attending our church. He seemed proud and enjoyed himself, and I felt myself grow stronger and even more sure of my new path.

We gathered in circles, hand in hand, and prayed together. We prayed for the sick, for those trapped in the vicious cycle of addiction, and we encouraged people who had lost all hope. We started creating a buzz, and our numbers grew week by week as we sang and pounded on African drums for rhythm. I played the guitar and sang. I have to admit, I wasn't the best guitarist you'd ever heard, but that didn't stop us from celebrating, night after night.

But, like a constant niggling whisper in the back of my mind, I couldn't stop feeling the underlying guilt about my obvious personal double standards, and I really started to question my long-term involvement in the drug business.

I had been told over and over again about God's mercy and unconditional forgiveness, regardless of my actions, but I soon realized that didn't do my morality - or lack thereof- any favors. I'd convinced myself that as I was using the drug money to fund the church and only doing good things with it, surely God would forgive me for importing the drugs? Surely it was better for the profits to support spreading the word of God rather than supporting the criminal underworld? I never went near the product myself anymore, so surely God's mercy would cleanse me.

But I still couldn't shake the doubt, and the July that summer marked a real turning point in my life.

Our group had decided to go to an annual Christian convention together. It was held out in the countryside. I immediately felt a resistance to going, as if something was trying to prevent me from attending. But my inner rebel won, and I decided to go anyway. We drove up that Wednesday, and as we arrived, I unexpectedly caught sight of the Chief Superintendent of the entire Icelandic police force. I felt sick to my stomach as he approached us.

"It's amazing what you guys are doing here," he said. "May I join you for one of your meetings?"

I was flabbergasted.

"Sure." I gulped back my surprise. "In fact, why don't you come up and speak?"

When the Thursday evening gathering arrived, we praised God, and the worship began with the same energy and excitement as we always had during our home meetings. We'd gathered a large crowd, and then, to my huge surprise, sure enough, the Chief Superintendent came up to the stage and took the mic!

My head was spinning. Here I was, sharing the same space as the very people who had once been my prosecutors and had imprisoned me all those years ago. I felt something shift inside me, but the most life-altering moment was still to come. Feeling inspired, I stood up and took the microphone during the 'call for prayer' requests - when all of a sudden, an Icelandic phrase I'd heard dropped into my mind:

"You can't stand on two rocks; you have to choose your path."

The words echoed through my mind, and in an instant, without question, I knew what I needed to do. I couldn't continue serving God with one hand while selling drugs with the other. There was no doubt about it; I finally had to walk away from it all.

I was done.

As soon as I got home, I called a meeting with my business partners and told them that I wanted out. I had a shipment worth a huge amount of money on the way, but I made it clear that I no longer wanted any involvement. I wanted nothing to do with it. They could keep my share of the profits. My experience at the convention had been so powerful and transformative that I never looked back.

I explained everything to Denni that night.

"Aren't you taking this whole integrity thing a little bit too seriously, man?" he asked, not at all pleased with my change of direction.

"I mean, what about the sign on the building?!"

I laughed. On the ground floor of our building was a business called 'Best', which sold cleaning products. The word 'Best' was displayed in three places outside. 'Best! Best! Best!'. We had always found it hysterical and got a real kick out of it because we were known for having the best cocaine.

"Denni, there's really no going back for me. I just want to do what's right."

I stuck to my guns, put my front man in contact with my business associates and left without a second thought.

That same summer of 2007, we opened another church in my hometown of Keflavik. Things were booming, and it seemed to be a season of amazingly serendipitous encounters. One such encounter was with Kristian, the director of the local Pentecostal church, a man whose open-mindedness would forever change my journey. I bumped into him unexpectedly and decided, on the spur of the moment, to ask him if we could hold our services and meetings in his church hall under our own name, "Love." I was stressed out that he'd say no, but he called a few days later with an enthusiastic yes!

I was walking on air; my fellowship group would now have a second branch, and in my hometown, no less!

He had believed in me.

Letter from Kristian- Pastor of the Pentecostal Church, Keflavik.

I'd been working in Christian ministry for more than 20 years and knew, all too well, that it was one thing to accept Christ and another to continue to live with him. I'd seen so many men like Baldur be saved only to return to their old lives. But Baldur reached out to me again to use the church, and somehow, an inexplicable compulsion led me to say yes!

Not long after, the Saturday evening gatherings grew, and a new worship group was formed on the spot. There was a sudden influx of new souls from as young as 14 years, yet our faithful core group remained the same. The gatherings were bursting with joy and song, and the pulpit welcomed all kinds of speakers, offering diverse and interesting perspectives.

Then their baptisms began! I can't even begin to count how many people we baptized, but on one memorable occasion, the uncontained joy of the moment led to the baptismal pool overflowing and completely flooding the assembly hall. I received a frantic phone call from a young man, asking me what to do – "Just turn off the water!" I shouted over the phone, but somehow that went wrong too, and the crazy celebration continued amidst the water until I got there and turned it off myself!

It's one of those moments that is really only funny in retrospect.

It's safe to say that Baldur's group touched many lives and more than lived up to its name—Love. The young man that this book is about still walks with God fourteen years later and is a true testament to the fact that God can transform people's lives.

His words truly touched my heart.

Love had indelibly changed the course of my life.

I was no longer a devious, manipulating drug dealer; I was no longer chased by dark shadows of fear. I had become a channel for the divine love of the heavenly Father.

He was simply the Best.

Part 3

24
TEARING DOWN THE WALLS

Throughout my life, dreams have often inspired or pre-empted some of my most significant experiences, both good and bad. In the earlier chapters of my life, I had often ignored them, but by my late twenties, I had come to realize that these nocturnal messages were, more often than not, worth paying real attention to.

The story of my mother's dream and tearing down the walls that once concealed my past life is something I can't ignore.

In 2006, my mom had been living in an apartment in the same building as mine. The very same apartment that we had used as the brothel in previous years. She had recently come out of another stint in rehab and was battling her own demons, so I offered her the space to be close to me while she recovered.

One morning, as I was on my way out, she ran up to me, desperate to share a dream she had had the night before.

The timing of this dream was nothing short of remarkable.

"I had a wonderful dream about the apartment, Baldur," she said, her voice trembling with excitement. "It had been turned into a beautiful big open hall filled with light. There were no walls inside it anymore, and Baldur... it had been converted into a church!"

My curiosity stirred. "Mom, I was literally on my way out now to pick up blueprints of the building. I'm applying for a permit to install a balcony. This is weird!"

I drove to the city offices, and in no time, I held the blueprints in my hands, the faded ink revealing a forgotten history. I was blown away - the apartment, it turned out, had originally been designed as a church auditorium. An excited shiver ran down my spine, and I drove home to tell my mom. I immediately knew what had to be done. I had to restore the space to its original purpose. Its former glory. I buzzed with a new sense of purpose and conviction.

I also realized that a monumental task lay ahead. This apartment had witnessed the complete depths of my dark past and had many of my shameful secrets concealed within its walls. We'd made some changes to the place when we'd used it as a brothel and drug lair and had added iron reinforcements to the front door so that the cops would have a hard time breaking through it. Now, those very same walls would need to be broken down, and the scars of my past would be revealed.

And so, we were all in, and our fellowship group embarked on our new journey and got straight to work on tearing down the walls. We had totally outgrown our space anyway, with people sitting on windowsills, crowding the doorway, and even standing out in the hallway for our meetings.

As we delved deeper into our renovation project, a trove of forgotten memories was unearthed, each item a stark reminder of my former life of hidden drugs and money, stashed away like a guilty conscience. Mom found all kinds of dubious things as she helped clean the place out. But, strangely enough, as each brick was removed, I felt lighter, and what emerged from beneath the rubble was perfect - a beautiful, oblong-shaped hall bathed in light. Our new lectern, which had previously been the brothel bar, was sanded and glossed up and looked ironically perfect.

As the day of our opening service approached, we also invited Jonathan, the chief superintendent of the Icelandic police force, who'd preached at the festival, to come and speak. We found it appropriate since he'd been a guard during my time inside and was such a personality. The service finally started, and we raised our voices, singing rearranged old Icelandic hymns - the joy was palpable! Johnathan, a man whose life path had crossed mine in the most unexpected way, spoke passionately about God's boundless love. The service was fantastic! It was described as fresh, innovative, and completely unpretentious, which was very important to me. An article in a local newspaper was headlined: "Whore House Converted to a House of Prayer." It's not your usual news story. We had found light in the darkest of places.

Ice and Fire

Things moved on full steam ahead. We had built so much in such a short space of time, and in the end, I inevitably decided to give up my job and devote myself full-time to the church. It would require everything of me.

As the walls of my past had crumbled, so too did the ones within my heart.

25
PUNCHING OR PRAYING

Let the past remain in the past.

Those who do not remember the past are condemned to repeat it.

We all have a past, and whether we like it or not, the past leaves an indelible mark on our present. A sometimes-haunting reminder of poor choices made.

As my work in the church started, I realized that redemption was not going to be a straightforward journey but a constant negotiation with the past.

One Friday that first autumn, as the late afternoon sun filled our new church hall, I was preparing for a meeting when the sound of the doorbell suddenly pierced the air, jolting me from my work. Surprised, I stood up, opened the bulletproof inner door, and walked down the stairs to open the front door.

Standing outside on the street, in what was obviously an extremely unsettled, angry, and altered state, was my really good friend and faithful 'Strong Arm´ from the old days, Axel.

He was clearly very, very upset.

Ice and Fire

"You're betraying me!" Axel shouted loudly and hysterically, his eyes wild with distress.

"What? What do you mean, Axel?" I was totally taken aback.

He was clearly experiencing some kind of psychotic drug-induced episode. His eyes narrowed, and he suddenly made a move to attack me. His intentions were very clear. I quickly moved my right leg back and positioned my hands to react, trying to balance myself so that if I had to, I could get to him before he managed to get a blow at me.

"Why are you betraying me?!" he growled furiously, white froth dripping from the corners of his mouth.

I had never seen him like this before.

"Axel…why would I betray you?" I asked as gently as I could, trying to diffuse the horrible, volatile situation. We stood face to face, teetering on the edge of a seriously violent encounter right outside the church. My mind raced. I knew that I had to put an end to this immediately, and if I had to, I would throw the first punch. Violence would be my last resort, though.

As I continued to try and reason with him, suddenly a very clear image flashed through my mind. The memory of a story I had heard about a famous preacher from the Bronx in New York. When a gang of ghetto boys had stormed into his church, roughed him up, and attempted to steal the collections box…the preacher just stood in the doorway and prayed for them. They pulled knives on him, threatened to slice him open, to kill him, but he simply remained steadfast, standing in the church's doorway, calmly praying, resolute in his commitment to his faith.

Now, it was my turn. I knew what I needed to do. Instead of letting my clenched fists fly in Axel's face, I placed my right hand on his chest, closed my eyes and started to pray. I used all of the strength I could muster, and as I spoke, I felt Christlike love begin to replace the hostility in the air.

Slowly but surely, Axel simmered down as I just stood there, embracing him. Then, he breathed out a long, shivering sigh. It was as if all the wind had been knocked out of this big, burly, sensitive brute.

"Jesus loves you," I said. "And…so do I."

He looked down at his feet, turned around, and vanished into the darkness. Not another word.

Although Axel and I were really good friends, he was always completely unpredictable whenever he was using, which made me wary. He often became extremely paranoid, and in the past, I'd seen deep cuts all over his hands. Fueled by chemically induced anxiety and rage, he'd always slept with a kitchen knife under his pillow. Always prepared.

Ice and Fire

After the incident, I decided it was time to invite Axel to join our group. "I already have faith, Baldur," he replied.

I tried again, but he declined my invitation…and slowly, he disappeared from my life.

Later, I would learn that Axel had brutally attacked someone and had been sent to prison…which had led to the ultimate tragedy -

Axel took his own life.

This sad news weighed heavily on my soul, and I couldn't help but wonder if I could have done more for him. The night I encountered Axel on the precipice of despair is forever etched in my memory. Our friendship was forged on our shared past struggles, and I was the one who had survived them. It was a hard lesson, but I decided right there and then that in moments of confrontation, I would now always choose prayer over violence.

Compassion over vengeance.

My past had already claimed too much.

My cousin Denni was another person who was confused, as well as openly amused by my new lifestyle and choices. He was still struggling with his own battle with addiction, and it often felt like he watched my transformation with a mixture of skepticism and curiosity. I tried to persuade him to just give it a try and give everything to God, but he had an unserved prison sentence hanging over him that he was deeply dreading, and he was reluctant and unconvinced that anything could change for him.

One day, after another of our usual deep discussions, Denni and I had a falling out, and he stormed off and left, annoyed. He ignored all of my attempts to contact him. I was used to this kind of reaction from him, so I thought nothing of it.

The next morning, on the 17th of December 2007, Denni went to the cemetery... and hanged himself.

I was at home when I received the devastating and sickening news. The weight of the most horrific sorrow and heavy guilt bore down on me. I was lost. I had never dealt with tragedy stone-cold sober before, and it was a stark reminder of my ongoing, relentless battle between the light and dark within me. I had chosen my side, though, and it was a battle I was determined to fight, no matter the cost.

In a fit of anguish and determination, I leaped to my feet. I could no longer stand by and watch the past claiming the lives of the people I loved. I was done. I simply couldn't deal with the idea of returning to my mundane job, constructing iron reinforcements for concrete floors, with this ever-increasing weight on my shoulders. I met with my boss and quit my job, fueled by the desire to somehow make sure that no one else would ever have to succumb to the same fate that had claimed my dear friend and my cousin. It was time for action.

26

BE NOT AFRAID

As the numbers and the reputation of our beautiful new church grew, so did mine, and suddenly, I found myself thrust into the spotlight.

Reporters from the Icelandic State Broadcastings Service visited our church, and before long, I was interviewed live on a Christian TV show. It was a surreal experience, and sitting in that TV studio, under the glare of the lights and the gaze of the camera, I thought about everything that had brought me to that moment.

I opened up and spoke from the heart. I told the truth about my former life, my addictions, my prison time, running the brothel, and the hope that had pulled me out of the abyss. My grief over Denni's suicide had brought me even closer to God and even more determined to help and rescue others, so just before the interview ended, without giving it a second thought, I announced live on air –

"And…we'll be holding a prayer walk on November 10th!" Perhaps I had been a little too impulsive.

I gulped.

November was only a month away, and in my usual hyperactive enthusiasm, I hadn't even taken the time to check if that date was suitable. I had a knot of anxiety and excitement in my stomach when the interview was over. I wanted to start a revolution.

So, now, in a bit of a pinch because of my eagerness, we decided we had to meet every morning to hash out the details and get this 'prayer walk' planned. The blank canvas of our planning board stared back at us, waiting for inspiration to strike. And it did! As my team and I brainstormed, my panic began to fade. Honestly, we didn't have a cent to our name, but still, we outlined routes, created a list of volunteers, and started organizing the massive event. Slowly but surely, my impetuous, crazy announcement started to feel like a real plan.

We decided to get people from every church in the country to collaborate with us to promote unity among the Christian community in Iceland. In the weeks that followed, we worked constantly and tirelessly, but the stress of the impending prayer walk weighed on me heavily. As always, I turned to prayer and sought solace in the pages of the Bible, but my fear and that little nagging inner critic started to get the better of me.

"You can't do this – you're just some drug dealer trying to pretend he's in control..."

Doubt and anxiety started looming over me, casting a shadow on the faith that had brought me so far.

Ice and Fire

As November 10th inched closer, in a huge leap of faith, we decided to rent Laugardal Hall, a massive events center in Reykjavík. We were determined to host a huge concert there after the walk, even though we were almost completely out of pocket. The church had rallied the support of Iceland's Police Superintendent, which was a significant step, but with all the profound changes happening in my personal life, I found myself in an ironic situation. My personal fears started to niggle at me again.

There I was, a former criminal - now deeply involved in a wholesome

Christian project with the police superintendent of all of Iceland by my side. The Superintendent even confided in me about the criticism he had faced for supporting me. A few members of the police force had warned him against me, believing that I was using this opportunity as yet another scheme to engage in criminal activities.

My personal transformation had been so dramatic, that even I began to doubt my own worthiness.

I knew I needed a break. A moment of quiet to reconnect with my faith. Jonathan, my steadfast friend who had always been there for me, invited me to stay on his farm in the eastern part of Iceland. For an entire weekend alone, I did nothing but pray... and pray some more. Then, on a Sunday night, I went to a gathering at Jonathan's place to join a prayer meeting. The meeting blasted off with a wave of beautiful, uplifting music, and a sense of weightlessness and freedom that I hadn't felt in a long time washed over me the minute I started singing along.

I smiled as I was reminded of the time one of the guards at the prison had caught me singing in the prison shower.

"I've never heard anybody singing in this shower before!" he'd laughed with a confused look on his face.

"Well...I wonder why that is?" I smiled. "This place doesn't exactly inspire joy, does it?"

Despite any lack of occasion for the song in prison, singing still energized me, as it always had. Singing always transported me and helped me forget time and place. By closing my eyes and singing aloud, I could escape somewhere else, far away from that godforsaken place.

At that prayer meeting that Sunday night in the countryside, I closed my eyes and just sang. Longing to draw nearer to God. It was during this profound moment of reflection that, for the first time ever, I saw an image of Jesus in my mind.

"Don't be afraid, Baldur," he said. "I am with you."

Ice and Fire

I heard a voice echo inside me, and the words held so much reassurance that I could no longer contain my emotions. Tears started flowing down my cheeks. I wasn't used to crying, especially in front of others…but this moment was different.

Then, of course, my inner critic kicked in: "Come on, Baldur. You're just imagining things, and you're probably embarrassing yourself!"

But…the same phrase kept echoing through my mind - "Don't be afraid, Baldur. I am with you."

That night, a new, blinding truth hit me. I no longer had to protect myself. Jesus Christ wanted to protect me. Jesus was my refuge. My shield. I almost instantly felt my doubts wash away, and as I opened my eyes, I realized that my overwhelming anxiety was gone as well.

Now, I was ready for the walk.

I got back to Reykjavik, rejuvenated and full of energy. Our prep for our event was well underway, and we also decided to visit every high school in the country as a promotion. We held meetings in school cafeterias, and I would jump onto tables and animatedly share my story. I told them how God had released me from the darkness, and we offered to pray for anyone who wanted it. Of course, I was nervous about how know-it-all teenagers might respond, but we were beyond grateful to see how many of them were deeply moved and stood up to join us.

As our big event got closer, opportunities just seemed to open up for me to talk about my newfound freedom. A broadcaster from a Christian radio station even invited me to record a song in their incredible studio, and as someone who had always had a deep love of music and had on many occasions felt its transformative power - this was a dream come true.

Then, the day of our prayer walk arrived. I was stressed, to say the least! I couldn't help but worry if anyone would even show up! Standing in front of Hallgrim's Church, one of Iceland's most beautiful and famous churches, I felt a mix of massive relief and pure joy as groups of people started streaming towards us. By 2 pm, thousands of people were ready and waiting, and we set off on our prayer walk together.

It was better than I could ever have imagined! The procession was led by four police motorcycles, followed by swarms of people from various clubs and organizations. The Scouts also marched along, and the Salvation Army's International staff band played. I sang into a megaphone as we made our way through the streets, inspired and full of hope. Looking back, I could see that the crowd stretched all the way to our starting point, and the town square in front of the parliament building was also packed with people.

Ice and Fire

We stood up together on the platform and started the service, and as we sang, the power of our unity and harmony was overwhelming - three thousand voices joined together in song. I was privileged to end the evening by sharing my personal story of how God's power had transformed my life.

Standing up there that night in front of thousands, I couldn't help but think about the story of David and Goliath and how it suddenly really resonated with me. As I looked out at the crowd, I realized that I'd finally found a sense of purpose. I had often found myself in David's shoes, facing my own giant of a past, but that evening, the giant lay lifeless on the ground.

Defeated.

My battle for real change had truly begun.

27

THE RESTORATION

It's often said that when God provides the vision, he also provides the provision. I carried this unwavering belief with me as I led our new congregation. I had to. We really didn't have much, but every time we found ourselves in need, it seemed God delivered.

Like the day I met Graham. I'll never forget it. He and his wife Selma had visited our new church, and after one of our meetings, he walked up to me, smiling.

"I noticed you don't have many chairs, Baldur," he remarked. "How many do you need?"

"Ha! About a hundred," I smiled back.

Without a moment's hesitation, he nodded and simply said, "Great. I'll have them delivered to you later today."

I felt an instant connection with him and could tell right away that this man obviously possessed a keen business sense as well as a tremendous willingness to do good. As we hauled all the chairs up the stairs later that very same day, I couldn't help but be astonished. Graham had attended just one meeting, seen what we needed, and generously delivered without expecting anything in return. The new chairs were cool and stylish and gave our congregation hall a great new look. I was filled with gratitude.

With each passing day, excitement grew, more and more people joined our church gatherings, and it wasn't long before the room became too small and cramped once again. People stood in the doorway, leaned against walls, and even sat in the stairwell. The Icelandic National Television Service even contacted me and broadcast a short news segment about our church's remarkable transformation.

However, despite our newfound success, I was still emotionally very raw, and the shadows of my previous life still lingered. This is where kind people like Graham and his wife, Selma, proved to be a gift beyond measure. Their unwavering support served as a constant reminder of my new identity. They were selfless and accepted me as if I were their own son. Their love gave me the strength to keep going in the face of my still ongoing adversity, and it also motivated me to seek reconciliation with those I had wronged. My past still haunted me daily, but I was determined that I wouldn't let it stop me.

After a lot of back and forth and soul searching, I decided the time had come to reach out to the sister of the young man who had tragically passed away after the traumatic incident that fateful night in Reykjavik many years before. The biggest mistake and shame in my life that weighed on me more profoundly than any mere words could ever express.

Her name was Margaret. I contacted her and asked if she would meet me.

She accepted.

My anxiety was through the roof as I sat waiting outside Graham's house for her to arrive. I had decided meeting her close to them would maybe give me a sense of security and comfort.

My nerves were shot. What could I possibly say to this girl?

The moment she drove up and I saw her number come up on my phone, I nearly passed out. I felt sweat trickle down my forehead, and my breathing became so rapid and shallow that I felt like I was suffocating. I was afraid my legs would simply give out when I finally managed to stand up. Could I even manage to walk over to her car? I was so consumed with shame and remorse that all I wanted to do was run away and hide. Summoning every ounce of strength I had, I managed to make my way to the passenger's side door and sit down inside, fighting back my tears.

The weight of my guilt made it impossible to find words, but I eventually mustered up the courage to speak, my voice quivering with shame.

Ice and Fire

"Hi, Margaret," I said softly. "Hi," she replied.

The air was thick and heavy with tension.

"Margaret, I just wanted to tell you how terrible..." My voice cracked as I held back tears. "How... terrible I feel about what I've done to you. To you and your family."

My voice broke as I struggled to express the magnitude of my remorse. I wanted to cry, but I restrained myself because I didn't want to look as though I was searching for pity.

"I know... everything I say feels so... insignificant, so meaningless compared to the hurt I've caused you..."

Margret was silent.

"I know that there's nothing...nothing... I could ever say or do to make up for what I took from you."

The silence was deafening.

"I just want you to know that I will devote my life to making amends for my actions...but still...every day, I wish I could do something to make it all better."

I felt sick.

After what felt like the world's longest eternity, Margaret turned to me and quietly said:

"Baldur, you're doing your best to take responsibility for this."

Then, the most beautiful words… "I forgive you."

This time, I allowed the tears to flow.

"Margaret, I really don't know what to say. Thank you. Thank you from the bottom of my heart."

When I left her car, I felt as if the most colossal weight imaginable had been lifted from my shoulders. I was so shaken that I couldn't complete a single thought, but a voice inside me whispered, "You have been pardoned, and if you forgive others, I will restore you."

Could God really restore me in spite of my horrific mistake and the shame that had defined and shaped me ever since?

Thanks to Margaret's grace and selfless kindness, the process of my personal restoration took its first beautiful step.

28

A HUG FROM DAD

"Baldur, how would you like to come with me to Canada?"

Sitting at the kitchen table at Graham and Selma's place one night, shortly after meeting Margaret, Graham asked me a question that would change everything.

"Wow, I'd be up for that. Sounds amazing!" I reacted instantly.

He told me it would be his treat and he would pay for the whole trip. I stood there quite baffled. I just wasn't used to people doing things like that for me without expecting something in return. I felt slightly embarrassed but so grateful and thanked him profusely. He registered us for a course in Canada that was scheduled to start in January 2008. The director of a humanitarian organization called 'Symbiosis,' a guy named Hendrik, joined us too, and soon, we were on our way.

We landed in Toronto, filled with anticipation. After the first full, exciting day of the program, the three of us went out to eat. Graham took a seat in the booth closest to the wall, and Hendrik, who was a former police officer, motioned for me to slide in first beside Graham. This meant that I'd be trapped between the two of them.

I looked Hendrik in the eye.

"No custodian of the law is ever going to lock me in again," I said, straight-faced. "You get in first; I'm sitting on the end."

He stared at me, dead serious, and I watched him straight-faced as it eventually dawned on him that I was just messing with him. He took the joke well and we all had a good laugh.

It suddenly struck me that I must have really stuck out like a sore thumb in the group. There I was in Toronto, with a prosperous businessman and a former cop, taking part in a three-week Bible school course. It was comical. I mean, it would have been completely understandable if people had assumed I was under their watch; I was still quite rough around the edges and unpolished, to say the least, next to these esteemed and respectable gentlemen. Let's just say it was obvious that we were not of the same ilk. They kept a quiet, low profile, and I tended to be loud, outgoing, and I definitely stood out as the center of attention in most places I went...but I think they enjoyed that.

The course was extraordinary. It began with a lesson on how to hear God's voice - how to listen for it. I found the subject extremely interesting and actually quite straightforward. My negative inner voice came from my internal enemy, and the quiet, loving, encouraging one I was hearing more and more often belonged to God.

Next up was the subject of God's fatherly love. I listened closely as the speaker confirmed that I was a child of God and that my Father's everlasting love for me was real. I realized that I understood this on an intellectual level but not on an emotional one. He taught us about the difference between knowing something intellectually and experiencing it emotionally. I was lost. Even with all of my experience of immense pain, I couldn't understand the difference. I knew, though, that God loved everyone, and that gave me the hope of escaping from the darkness of my disturbed past.

Then, one morning on the course, a man named Ed Piorek swept into my life. He was an older man, a really well-spoken, enigmatic figure with long grey hair, from California. He had a quiet, unassuming type of wisdom that set him apart from the people I had heard speak so far. He spoke slowly and obviously, his words separated by long, intense pauses. It was as if he was keeping an eye on whatever was happening within the room while he taught, completely aware of and open to all of our energies.

I was quite spellbound.

Ed's presence, though, was a double-edged sword for me. As he kept talking, I felt his words stir something inside me, and I had no idea what it was. I was suddenly overwhelmed by emotion, and I found it nearly impossible to concentrate. In the spaces between his words and sentences, my mind raced, and my heart started to beat uncomfortably. I was captivated, but soon, I realized it wasn't just admiration I was feeling; it was something far deeper. Something confusing and honestly, quite disconcerting.

As this turmoil of unfamiliar emotions poured over me, I was so uncomfortable in my own skin, suddenly, that I even left the room to find some quiet. But even then, this strangely intense feeling of enormous admiration for him still overwhelmed me.

I threw my hands in the air in a desperate plea. What was going on? Had I fallen in love with a man?

I was completely confused. I waited for a moment, then decided to go back down to the auditorium and slunk back into my seat. It was then that I became aware of a quiet, tender voice deep inside me.

Just a whisper.

"My precious son, what you are feeling is the love that I have for you."

My tears began to flow. Tears of joy. It was as though I had been lost my whole life, and I had finally arrived home. It seemed too good to be true. Could it be possible that with all my flaws and past mistakes, I was actually cherished by God? I'd hurt people, mocked God and his followers, and turned my back on him so many times.

Could it really be that I was loved unconditionally?

I thought about my lifelong battle for the right to exist. I thought about the effort I'd put into gaining approval and finding some kind of purpose. The love I experienced in that moment was so overpowering that I had no words. I couldn't even express myself.

For the first time in my whole life, I was filled with complete inner peace.

In that calm and beautiful instant, I had a new understanding of the gospel. Jesus was the way to the heart of the Father and had come to build the bridge between us. I had heard that so many times but never really felt it. The intense love that I was feeling was me finally reuniting with my real Father - God.

After the course, Graham and Hendrik invited me on a day trip to Niagara Falls, but instead, I decided to stay and take part in a program called 'In the Stillness.' I sat in silence for two days. Me - the guy who could barely sit still for a minute without saying something! I felt transformed, and in the quiet of those two days, I realized that the only thing we really deeply desire, above all, is to be loved and to love in return.

Those three weeks in Toronto marked a profound change in my life, but even with all of the personal growth and revelations, I realized I still had a long way to go. The instructors at the school warned us to be patient and understand that it was a process. Our personal development was like the layers of an onion. You can choose to peel, slice or dice, and there are often tears involved.

Their analogy really touched me - just as an onion sheds its layers one at a time, we can slowly shed our old selves, allowing the real core of our being to emerge. Fresh and renewed.

I got back from Canada bright-eyed and bushy-tailed and ready to take on whatever challenges might come my way. I began each morning with a meditation I'd learned on the course. I would lie down on the floor and dedicate thirty quiet, undisturbed minutes to listening intently for the whispers of God. At the time, my friend Greg and I hung out a lot together, both being at the same point in our journeys. One day, while we were meditating together, I suddenly felt strangely compelled to go to the unlikeliest of places - the psych ward at the National Hospital.

"Uh…the psych ward?" Greg responded with an uncertain smile.

Following my gut, even though I was nervous, I somehow managed to convince him, and we got into the car. As we neared the hospital, though, doubts started creeping in. I realized If I went inside and said I'd "heard a voice," they'd probably lock me away as a patient on the spot.

Something inside me was completely determined though, and as we reached the entrance of the hospital psych ward, I spotted a young man walking towards us. An unexplainable nudge from inside prompted me to strike up a conversation with him.

"Hi, how are you doing, buddy?" "Huh? Me?"

His demeanor was uneasy, his eyes distant, and an aura of sadness surrounded him. After a few words, I decided spontaneously to invite him along on a drive. He accepted hesitantly, in spite of his obvious reservations; after all, I was a complete stranger. As we drove, I asked him questions to try to make him feel more comfortable. The darkness emanating from the poor guy was palpable. His name was Thor, and he told Greg and me that he'd tried to get himself admitted to the psych ward, but they had turned him away. He was renting a room in a hotel right in the city center.

At that moment, within the confines of a simple car journey, our paths converged.

"I was going to take my life," he uttered, exhausted. "I had a rope in my room. I was ready to go. Being admitted was my last resort."

Over the previous 6 months, he had gone to the psychiatric ward 6 or 7 times, and he had been on his way back to finally do it when he'd bumped into us. That was all the confirmation I needed. Everything was crystal clear. Without hesitation, I invited Thor to move in with me and join our church community. He accepted, and we went straight to the hotel and gathered up all of his belongings. Everything but the rope.

We took him under our wing, and he lived with us for nine months as a new member of our extended family. For as long as he could remember, Thor had struggled with the heavy burden of his childhood abuse alone, but within the nurturing embrace of our community, he found the courage to speak about everything that was haunting him. We worked hard and faced each of his challenges together. Step by step. Today, Thor is an amazing testament to the transformative power of God's love - a happily married man with a family of his own. His story was so wonderful, in fact, that he even became the inspiration for the halfway house that we established in our church, offering refuge to anyone seeking it. I was so thrilled for Thor and so proud. He gave us definitive proof that it is love that heals wounds, gives second chances, and rebuilds lives.

He was living proof of the life-changing effects of the Father's love. Or, as Thor called it – "A hug from Dad."

29

GOLD

With the church and the halfway house's success, word continued to spread like wildfire, and all sorts of people started flocking to our doors, from criminals to cops, Christians to Atheists, and addicts - a crazy blend of diverse and interesting souls exactly as we wanted it.

One day, we even invited a SWAT officer to come and speak for us. His name was Ivan. He stood tall and proud at the pulpit, right in front of the old brothel's former bar counter, and told the tale of Rahab, the Old Testament's transformational figure, who changed her ways by abandoning prostitution and following God. The irony wasn't lost on anyone, and I had to smile. Ivan, who had often visited the place in an official police capacity when it was a brothel, now stood in it preaching a message of change.

He continued on and declared proudly and without any explanation,

"I have been here many, many times in the past…but for a very different purpose!"

I had to stifle a giggle. His purpose remained a mystery, and for days after his speech, whispers and rumors started to circulate, and some of the guests concluded that he must have been a "patron" of the brothel. I tried as hard as I could to correct this misunderstanding whenever people came to talk to me, but I realized quickly that they didn't judge him, the truth or not. This open-minded attitude was exactly what I loved about the culture that characterized us as a group.

As our gatherings continued to swell, Graham, in his usual helpful way, approached me after a meeting that had been so packed that people could barely move.

"You know, Baldur, I think I know a good place for you. In fact, I've always thought it should be a church. Come with me. I'll show you!"

And just like that, a new chapter began. We drove down to the industrial side of the city, and Graham led me straight into the old boxing gym where I'd trained many years before. As I walked in, memories flooded my senses, and I could almost hear the thud of gloves on bags.

"You can use this space for free," he declared, grinning from ear to ear.

Once again, his generosity left me speechless! We rolled up our sleeves, got to work, and transformed the old gym into our new sanctuary. With room for several hundred people, it became the perfect place for our gatherings.

Ice and Fire

A few days after we opened, a man who was locally known as 'Sam Syringe' contacted me out of the blue. A seasoned street dweller and terrible drug abuser, he laid bare his struggle to me.

"Baldur, can you help me?" He was really desperate. "I can't keep this up any longer."

"Are you willing to give up everything and turn to God?"

"I'm not going to make it if I don't," he whispered, exhausted.

The weariness in his voice was palpable. "In that case, bring everything here as soon as you can. Your needles, your drugs, your syringes…all of it."

The next day, Sam handed over a bag containing his entire world, and I tossed it straight into the trash, right there and then, in front of him. He looked me nervously in the eye, then stepped into our church. Into a new program. Into his new life. We believed in him, and against all odds, Sam made it. For the first time in his life, he surrendered everything to God.

His story also sparked a crazy tidal wave of interest, and our halfway house started to become a refuge for the lost. We welcomed notorious delinquents, serious junkies, and people we found out on the streets who had lost everything. Our method was a very simple one - we would find anyone who needed real help, anyone desperate enough to sacrifice everything to heal. We would pick them up, feed and shelter them, and most importantly, introduce them to Jesus. Even though I was steadfast in my faith at the time, I was still incredibly controlling and desperate to make it work, so I didn't allow them to get away with any protest. They had to follow the path we had tried and tested. No questions asked.

Around this time, Jonathan told me about a young man, Chris, a former leader in the local Pentecostal church, who was now caught in an awful downward spiral. He'd lost his job, abandoned any faith, resumed heavy drinking and drugs, and was now a jacked-up computer addict who never left his attic apartment.

Johnathan was convinced that we could get him in and help him. I got his number and boy, did I persist. I simply kept returning to his flat and ringing his doorbell until shame couldn't keep him hidden anymore. He lay there, shaking and nursing a horrible hangover. Later, he told me that he thought the idea of returning to church was impossible, and the weight of his shame and embarrassment kept him hidden behind closed doors.

Our meetings became Chris's refuge, and he slowly shed his vices, one by one, and actually joined our operation and started working with us, standing beside me like a welcomed pillar of support.

We started a new program called 'The Disciple School'. The number of people who signed up for our program was incredible,

Ice and Fire

seeing as though we were basically complete rookies in the field. I aspired to be real, honest, and unpretentious, and suddenly, our reach extended to all of Reykjavik's rural communities, and we even started to get visitors from abroad - like my unforgettable friend from Nigeria, Felix.

When I met him, he had nowhere to stay, so I offered him a mattress in the kitchen, as at the time, we literally had no free space or beds. Felix was a really funny, entertaining character, and as he pretty much lived in the kitchen, he often cooked us delicious African stews, which all the guys gobbled down with gusto.

I took him touring and showed him around Iceland, and one day, as we drove him through a tunnel that passed under a fjord, Felix suddenly sat up straight and shouted, "No, no, no, man! You are driving into the earth. Are we going to hell?"

That same night, out in the countryside, he saw the Northern Lights dancing in the sky for the first time, and he put his hands up to his head in awe at the sight.

"Ooh! There must be a war in heaven!"

It was pure gold! Felix's observations were filled with the awe and confusion of someone experiencing the extraordinary for the first time, and it was wonderful. Felix was just one of many guests who came to visit us from abroad and ended up staying longer than expected. Every day with him, we witnessed the transformative power of the Gospel. A constant reminder that God sees into our hearts and that just like Jesus, anyone can look at a muddy puddle beyond the dark, murky surface and see the gold that God has hidden there.

30
TO FORGIVE

It was August 2009 when I experienced what had to be one of the most pivotal and cathartic encounters of my life.

It was a big Icelandic holiday weekend, and a group of us from our congregation decided to go down to the Christian festival being held that Saturday evening. When we arrived, the director of the church, who was hosting the event, approached me with an unusual request.

"Baldur, is it okay if I call you up to the stage tonight?" he asked. Curious, I said, "Sure. Why?"

"Emil's mother is here, and I want to pray for you."

My heart almost stopped. Emil was the young man whose name had been in my heart and on the tip of my tongue every day for years. The young man who had tragically lost his life and whose life had become inextricably intertwined with mine. Now, his mother was at the festival, and I was about to face her in a very public setting.

A rush of muddled thoughts flooded my mind. What could I possibly say to his mother? How could I face her in front of all of these people?

I knew that mere words couldn't possibly make up for the horrific loss I'd caused her. My thoughtless and reckless actions had led to the death of her son when he was in the prime of his life. Full of the same old dread and regret, the more I thought about what to say to her, the more powerless I felt. My useless words would never be able to alleviate the pain I'd inflicted on her and her family. Yet deep down, I felt some small sense of peace, and I knew that God was with me.

The assembly started with a concert, and to my relief, music filled the air. As the music went on, that sense of inner peace that had been igniting grew stronger, and in an instant, I decided to place my trust entirely in the hands of God. The same words guided and echoed inside of me as the music played.

"You are not your past. You are pardoned."

Then, the moment arrived, and the director of the church called me up to the stage. Emil's mother was already standing there, waiting. I was shaking. He spoke to the audience, setting the emotional tone for the moment.

"A mother stands here tonight opposite a man who caused her son's death."

A hush fell over the assembly. "She is here to forgive him."

Ice and Fire

In that instant, Emil's mother walked towards me, stopped in front of me, and, to my complete shock, in an act of selfless grace, took me into her arms.

We embraced.

Words tumbled out of my mouth, and I felt myself crumbling as I spoke into her ear. I used every word I could summon up to express my sorrow for the suffering and loss I'd caused her. Unspeakable suffering and loss that I could never atone for. I told her I was determined to spend the rest of my life helping others who were struggling.

"Baldur…I forgive you."

Her words took my breath away, and I felt freedom unlike anything I'd ever experienced. She and God had granted me a gift that I could never ever give to myself. The most valuable gift of my life - freedom from my past.

Tears poured down my face. I was completely undone.

Stepping down from the stage together, we looked out at the packed hall, at hundreds of eyes glistening with tears.

Emil's mother was later interviewed by a news site and told them:

"When I think back, I initially had no intention of forgiving. People had tried to get me to come to this convention for two years, knowing that he may be there. The third time I was asked, I decided to go. That Friday, I was invited to come up onto the stage to be prayed for. I knew that the man who had invited me knew my story, but I said no.

Then, on the Saturday, as we were getting ourselves ready - I heard a whisper in my ear.

I knew it was my son.

He said: "Mom, God and I have forgiven…now it's your turn." I carried this with me when I went to the assembly that night, and when the same man asked me to come up to the stage, I just said yes without hesitation. I went onto the stage, walked toward him, and we hugged each other. The perpetrator and me. He spoke into my ear, and I spoke into his. I was forgiving him."

"Wasn't it difficult?" the interviewer asked.

"Yes, my God almighty. When I came back down, I was shaking like a leaf. My nerves were completely shot."

Interviewer: "I should clarify that I was there that night, and it was the most beautiful moment I've ever witnessed."

Ice and Fire

That incredible night, I was relieved of my life's most heavy burden. Until that moment, the thought of bumping into Emil's mother had always filled me with utter dread whenever I left my front door. That fear had vanished, I was healing, and all of my troubles seemed so far away.

31

A SON IS BORN

By 2010, even though my work was going fantastically, I still had a long way to go in my personal life. Aspects of my old nature kept resurfacing, and my old patterns and familiar behaviors still kept tripping me up.

Especially my tendency to be a little controlling.

One day, Graham took me aside at the church for a private conversation, gently pointing out that I couldn't call on him for help by simply snapping my fingers.

"I do that?" I asked, embarrassed and genuinely surprised.

But I realized he was right. It wasn't intentional at all, but I could see how it must have come across. I had an old habit of snapping my fingers to get things done, and there was always someone ready to leap into action. This was something I could easily work on, but there were deeper issues that needed my attention, especially when it came to my personal relationships.

At that time, I was single and celibate, having separated from my girlfriend a while before. When we met, I was a pimp, a drug addict, and a hardened criminal, and by the time our relationship ended, she was dating a guy who had started a church, didn't drink, and suddenly believed in abstinence before marriage. It didn't work for her anymore, and I understood. I was so different that I even decided to delete all the porn I had, eradicate it from my life and embrace complete celibacy. As I sat in front of the computer and the dopamine rushed to my brain as I opened each image to delete, I realized that porn triggered the same feeling in my brain as snorting a line of coke did. I needed to be free of it all.

Just in time for the most ironic twist of fate - a beautiful woman who used to work as a model started coming to our meetings. I was soon smitten, and despite Jonathan's caution about our differing paths, I dove headfirst into a relationship with her; so much for my vow of chastity.

Before we knew it, she was pregnant. Our relationship had been rocky from the start, but in my childlike faith, I believed that tying the knot would magically solve our issues. So, we got married that summer when she was several months along. Far from vanishing, though, our problems only got worse. I basically lived out of my gym bag; we fought like cats and dogs, and I began spending more and more nights at my mom's house.

Not surprisingly, these marital problems prevented me from flourishing at church. I'd chosen a woman whom none of the people closest to me would have chosen for me. I'd done it for all the wrong reasons, and everyone knew it. Graham and Selma were my rock during this time, and their love and support kept me from just giving up completely.

But a ray of light broke through on January 15th, 2010. The day my son came into the world.

The sheer joy of holding him in my arms was overwhelming. I cried tears of joy in the maternity ward as I cradled my beautiful baby boy, and in that moment, I almost literally felt my heart expanding to make room for all the love I had for my son. It sparked a glimmer of hope in me – maybe things would change for the better now that we were parents. They didn't.

We fought, the marriage deteriorated, and my wife started drinking again.

Things came to a head when she arrived home very late one night, and we started arguing, ending with her attacking me while I was holding our seven-month-old son. I managed to turn my back to her, but she punched, kicked, and clawed at me until I ran into a bathroom and locked myself inside. Even though it was the middle of the night, I called Graham in a panic and told him I didn't dare leave the bathroom. If I did, I was afraid I'd do something terrible by mistake. I called the police as well, and they arrived around the same time as Graham did. I felt almost silly calling the police over a domestic dispute, but I didn't know what else to do, locked in there with my son crying in my arms. Also, that was not the only time in the course of our relationship that I had locked myself in a room to get away from a bad situation.

Our marriage dissolved once and for all when our son was one year old. I'd always come running back, but by that point, I'd had enough. I had fought for my marriage as hard as I possibly could. I moved out with a gym bag full of my clothes, feeling like a loser. Here I was, dreaming of traveling the world and preaching, and I'd even made a mess of my own marriage.

Then, the issue of custody arose. For a while, it seemed like the best I could hope for was to be a weekend dad. Then, I received a summons to court for the custody assessment. As I opened the letter, my anxiety was off the charts, and the only thing I could think to do was pray. I knew that there was almost no chance that I would get custody because of my rocky past.

As I prayed, my anxiety gradually lifted, and that voice that I had become more and more accustomed to hearing inside me assured me.

"I will give you the words to speak."

The battle for the custody of my son would take a massive toll on me. My son was my everything, and this was only the beginning.

32

HEY, LITTLE SISTER

In 2011, I found myself divorced, depressed, still fighting a nasty custody battle, and taking care of my son solo. During that time, my mom was sober and doing really well, so I moved in with her. She provided valuable support in caring for my son while I was at work. On top of my church work, I had landed an extra job in sales at a call center and was feeling optimistic about my future in general. On my first night at the job, I exceeded the combined sales of the entire department. It felt great that the job suited me well and that I could make good use of my experience.

Before long, I found myself thriving in my new role and overseeing a sales team of nearly thirty people. I'd been helping others only on a volunteer basis since getting sober and was nervous about entering the job market, but finally, I was back in the game.

Then, out of the blue, tragedy struck.

I was in a jewelry store at the mall when my phone rang. It was around noon on the 30th of April 2011.

"Hello, Baldur. This is the police. We're with your mother. Can you come over right now?"

"What's the matter with her?" "Please come now."

Ice and Fire

I was frustrated. Sick and tired of getting involved in my mom's mess. I thought she had probably just been drunk and got into some trouble, The police officer insisted. "Baldur, you must come now. This is very serious!"

His voice was heavy.

"Okay, I'm on my way," I said reluctantly.

I was met at home by a priest and a police officer. I knew then. Someone was dead.

"Who is it?"

The weight of the moment bore down on me as I stood with the priest, waiting for an answer. It was then that I saw my mom. I'd often seen her cry, break down, and collapse under the strain of all kinds of abuse, trauma, and stress, but I'd never seen her like this before.

"Hanna," she sobbed. "She's dead…"

The words hit me like a freight train. "What? How?"

I let out a wail before anyone could answer. I stumbled into the next room, dazed, and pounded the wall. My little sister had just celebrated her 21st birthday the day before! It couldn't be true.

I tried to control my breathing.

Mom came into the room and said something, but my agony drowned out her words. I defaulted to the role I had always played within my family since I was a little boy. I approached the police officer, desperately seeking answers.

"I'm sorry. She was found dead from an overdose," he said. "She'd already died by the time the ambulance arrived."

"Hanna? An overdose…I don't understand…" My words hung in the air.

How could this happen to our family's brightest hope? Hanna, our amazing, accomplished soccer player in the national team. She had even just shared her plans to study psychology at the University of Iceland with me a few days before. I thought about the ring we'd given her, engraved with the phrase "Our Hero." She was our shining star. She had even embraced faith and started attending church with me.

Everything had been going so well.

Every time I inhaled, I felt a stabbing pain in my chest. How could my Hanna be dead?

Mom and my sister Sophie just stood there. Motionless. Their grief and hopelessness were palpable. I asked them if our brother David knew since he was working out in the countryside at the time. He didn't.

I called him.

"David... I need to tell you something..."

"What, Baldur? What's happened? Are you crying?"

"Yes ... she..."

What I didn't know was that David was at a restaurant at that very moment, reading a news article with the headline: 'Four arrested in connection with death in Árbær.'

"Is it Hanna?" "Yes..."

We wept together on the phone. My only wish was to take my little brother, who was several hundred miles away, into my arms.

"I'm coming home now," he whispered.

We called our nearest family members, and Mom and I headed to the hospital. I entered the chapel, where my little sister lay in the middle of the room. My closest family gathered around. My face was red with tears as I bent over her to kiss her forehead. When my lips touched her, I could feel that she was still warm. I wrapped my arms around Mom, who was shaking and weeping inconsolably.

When David arrived, his legs gave out from under him, and he fell to the floor, wailing.

I refused to accept that Hanna was gone. We started praying. I'd seen God perform such awesome miracles in my life and the lives of others. We had to have our miracle. Even Arnold, the priest from the state church, rose to his feet and joined in our prayer to raise her from the dead. We'd all read the stories in the Bible, and we'd heard that they still happened today.

It was unimaginably painful to see the desperation and hurt on the faces of all of my loved ones. We stood together and prayed for several hours until, eventually, all the blood had drained from Hanna's face.

She was as white as the sheet on which she lay.

I wept bitterly. I didn't understand how this could have happened. Why her, of all people? I wasn't aware that at that very moment, the young man who'd been accused of her death was in the room right beside the chapel.

Once I got home, in desperate need to find out what happened, I found out who had been arrested for killing Hanna and that she had been given homemade drugs. She was half-naked, and the guy responsible had been filming her. It had been her birthday party.

I also soon discovered that I had been put under heavy police surveillance, as the cops were convinced that I was going to take things into my own hands and teach the guy a lesson. I was being watched, but I wasn't given any information on her case as a matter of police confidentiality. A few days later, an old friend came to see me -

"Baldur, just let me take care of this; you shouldn't have to deal with it! I've got two foreign dudes on hand who can take care of the guy. Just nod your head, and they'll handle it."

I was so conflicted. A friend was standing in front of me, offering to avenge my little sister's death. I was overcome with grief, but at the same time, I'd devoted the last 3 years to preaching forgiveness, love, and restoration. My need for revenge won though, and at that moment, with my blood boiling and rushing through my ears, I nodded my head.

I gave the go.

The next day, I went out jogging, just as I used to every day with Hanna. While I was running, I suddenly felt as though Hanna was there beside me. I felt her presence. I felt her speak to me.

"Baldur, how do you want to remember me?"

I broke down in tears and stopped running. I desperately grasped for my phone, trembling, and called my friend.

"Don't touch him. Just leave him alone." I was met with a long silence on the other end of the phone.

"Baldur?"

"Just…don't touch him."

Later, as the perpetrator was sentenced and faced justice, I felt a small seed of compassion. I pictured a future visit to him in prison. I would see his remorse as I looked at him, I would embrace him in forgiveness, and I would give him an open invitation to come to our church. But for now, forgiveness was nowhere near.

For now, it was time to mourn Hanna's death.

The sight of her lying in a white coffin at the funeral left me breathless. I prayed to God to give me the strength at that moment to sing our song, a song I'd sung to her so often since she was a baby. I looked around at her nearest and dearest, stood before my little sister, and somehow, I sang.

After the service, someone came up to me and said, "Baldur, you should be proud. Where would your sister be if you hadn't chosen this path?" Then, it dawned on me. One single light in the darkness. I had led Hanna to faith. I had baptized her. Now, my beautiful sister was in heaven.

I would see her again. This was not a forever goodbye.

Then, we carried her out of the church and lowered her coffin into the earth.

Ice and Fire

Exactly one year later, to the day of Hanna's passing, the day of my son's custody hearing arrived. It had been an exhausting, yearlong battle, and I had never been so afraid in my life.

I sat in the courtroom and waited anxiously. The proceedings were delayed due to my ex-wife being late, but then she finally arrived, the judge entered, and the lawyers took their turns opening the hearing. The assessing psychologist, who had shown kindness to me, spoke some encouraging words about me as a father. Then, finally, at the end of her statement, my lawyer posed the most crucial question.

"Which parent do you consider most fit to take custody of the child?" The psychologist's response overwhelmed me with relief.

"I consider Baldur better suited for custody of the child."

"Though Baldur did accidentally cause a man's death, he has demonstrated, through the life he lives today, that he is not the same man he was before," the judge concluded.

I was awarded full custody.

I couldn't believe my ears. The judge's use of the word "accidentally" to describe the crime I committed contrasted completely with the judgment from my original trial when I was labeled a "thug with no extenuating circumstances." The legal system had finally recognized that I had not intended to take a life.

It was as if, suddenly, my past was being rewritten!

As I left the court that day, I remembered the words I had heard God speak to me when I took my first steps toward him. "You are not your past."

That glorious afternoon, they felt truer than ever.

33

BLESS THIS HOUSE!

After Hanna's passing, a period of great mourning followed. My heart was broken, and all of my dreams of traveling the world and sharing the message now seemed in tatters. Hanna had left a massive void in my life. My decision to forgive the man who had selfishly witnessed my sister's death without giving her any aid had not been an easy one and was one that I had to make again and again, day after day, for what seemed like an eternity. I was really hurting, and to add to that, I felt like I just couldn't hear God as well as I could before. I was frustrated.

Why could I not hear him now, during the most difficult time in my life?

I felt as though I had let my family, God, and the church down completely, and every day, my heart grew harder and more cynical. My mom was a mess, and the police were always calling me because she'd go off to get drunk and cause trouble. My sister Sophie was in visible anguish and had started drinking and having all sorts of awful family drama too. I was afraid for her and became worried that I would lose her as well. I tried my very best to do what I could for everyone and kept inviting them to meetings and church as a solace.

Even though I'd been a leader in the church for a long time, I was in a terrible state, so Graham and Selma suggested I take a break. I stood with my eyes closed at church one Sunday, listening to the music, when a friend of mine, Oliver (Who now runs the United Ministry, Iceland), approached me.

"Baldur, how would you like to come help me start United Reykjavík?" he asked. A missionary program designed to reach out to young people in the city.

I laughed at the thought. "You don't want me. Trust me." "Ok," he said, "but are you at least willing to pray about it?"

I agreed to pray on it, feeling insecure and closed my eyes again to concentrate on the music. He was going to have to wait; I was most definitely not in the right frame of mind for a new project. I would only let him down.

As I started to think about Oliver's question, though, a vivid sequence unfolded in my mind like scenes from a movie. I saw myself lying disoriented on the floor of a boxing ring. A huge, formidable opponent stood towering above me, taunting me. "You pathetic loser. You can't even stand. You destroy everything you touch. Just stay there on the floor, you black sheep!"

The wrestler continued his miserable mockery, but as I lay there on the floor, I suddenly heard a gentle, loving voice.

Ice and Fire

"Baldur, stand up. I love you."

I was immediately filled with raw emotion. Did God really still have faith in me? Was he urging me to take the chance and work with Oliver?

I opened my eyes and walked straight up to Oliver. "So, I think I might want to help you after all," I grinned. "I knew it!" he said excitedly, grabbing me in a tight hug.

We started our planning immediately and decided to start holding meetings at a theater downtown. The building we used was on a street in the East part of the city, surrounded by drug dens. A lot of people in the area weren't in a very good place in life. I felt my hope stir again. My hope is to live my life according to my calling to help others.

We had just started digging in to fix the place up when one of the guys from the street, named Tommy, came by to check it out. I knew Tommy from my previous attempts to support him in getting sober. He was quite the character.

"What are you guys doing here?" he asked eagerly. "We're moving the church here."

"A church!!" He smiled, tearing off his leather jacket, tossing it onto the floor, and stretching his hands up towards heaven.

"Dear Heavenly Father," he prayed joyfully and rather loudly. "Bless this house! May it be a wonderful blessing and a new hope to many! Amen!"

I felt tears well up in the corners of my eyes as I watched him smiling. He was shabbily dressed, quite smelly, and completely intoxicated, but who better to bless our new house? It seemed so serendipitous that he should come staggering in and pray for us, and we were both deeply touched. His prayer was answered too…in time, the church had an incredibly positive influence on the neighborhood. We helped many people, and the local junkies gradually became fewer and fewer in number, improving the general image of the area as a result as well.

It wasn't always smooth sailing, though. We had a lot of trouble and interesting incidents along the way. Like Andy, an active drug user, who joined us for a meeting one day. I noticed he'd left rather abruptly as the meeting started, only to find out afterward that he'd stolen the collection box. I knew that most drug deals in the neighborhood took place in a certain basement apartment on the street, and all the addicts hung around there, so I headed straight over there and knocked on the door. The man who greeted me was a long-time addict, and he recognized me instantly from the past, nodding.

"Is Andy here?"

"No," he replied, frowning.

"I know he's in there. Tell him to come out and talk to me."

He sighed and went back inside, where I heard him talking to Andy. Hunched over with shame, Andy stepped out of the door.

"Andy, where's the collection box?"

He shuffled his feet on the floor, ignoring me. I looked him straight in the eye.

"Andy, give me the box."

A brief silence followed, and then he slumped back inside to fetch it, muttering, "I suppose you want me to come out so you can beat me up." He came back out and looked at me, full of shame. He'd robbed the only people who'd always been ready and willing to help him.

"Andy, we love you, and I look forward to seeing you get sober again. You're always welcome at the church. This changes nothing between us, ok!"

I gave him a big hug and stood there holding him for a little while. He stood frozen, staring at me as I left, his face one big question mark. My response had taken him totally off guard. It wasn't long before he came to a meeting again, and we welcomed him with open arms.

The church was always open, so we had some real characters come and go at all hours. One night, a guy we called 'Prince Danny' came in and requested to see me. He'd been in prison at the same time as me, so I knew him vaguely. I came in to meet him, and we took a seat in the prayer room. He was very distressed and emotional. He sat and confessed every transgression he'd ever committed in his life to me. I was stunned. When he was finished, there was a short silence.

"Can God forgive me?" he asked.

Danny had been in prison ever since he was old enough to be locked up. He'd had a miserable childhood and really had very little hope for a normal life after the abuse he'd endured. He told me his whole story with such humility and bravery. I was very moved.

We prayed together for a while, and then he left. I found out later that he had died in prison. He was only one of many who died within the prison system because he hadn't received the appropriate help and support. I was really distressed about his death. Anger swelled up inside me, fueled by the injustice experienced by so many children born into dysfunctional families. Then, my anger turned into passion. A passion to champion those in society, too often cast aside and judged. Far too many people were trapped by their pasts, and it was time to do something about that.

Ice and Fire

But first, I had to confront my own past, and in an unexpected and wonderful twist, God sent a beautiful, remarkable woman to help me do just that.

34

I CHOOSE HIM!

Sometimes, what you need is right in front of your eyes; you only have to open them. It wasn't long before I met a woman. A woman who would change my life completely. A woman I would never have met had I not taken part in the Twelve Step program.

We had been in the same recovery group for years, but we had never caught one another's eye. She seemed to radiate calm and wholesomeness, and I suddenly found myself attracted to everything about her. Her blonde hair, infectious smile, and stunning presence were complemented by what seemed to be an inner wisdom and maturity that made me even more interested. Intrigued, I started to ask around about her. I found out that her name was Barbara; she was a single mom of six kids and was slightly older than I was.

One evening, while I was preaching at United Reykjavík, I caught a glimpse of her in the audience. After the meeting, I looked out for her and found her receiving prayer from a friend of mine. I decided to take a chance and approach her.

"Hi. Barbara? May I pray for you?" I asked her. She nodded, smiling.

From that moment on, I simply couldn't get her out of my mind. She was wonderful! A few days later, I took a leap of faith and decided to send her a friend request on Facebook. I waited nervously, hoping she'd accept.

To my delight, she did, and bumbling and not knowing what to say, I sent her a message under the guise of selling phone services (my day job at the time). I was pleasantly surprised when she replied, and we started chatting. The conversation flowed easily. Wary of my recent past and failed relationships, though, I was scared to get my hopes up too high. I decided to seek the advice of some friends who'd been in a successful marriage for many years. A wise person once told me that you don't go to a bankrupt man and ask him for financial advice. I opened up and had a great conversation with my friend Theo.

"Baldur, what are you waiting for?" he said, "She's mature, educated, manages a household with six children, and clearly knows where she's heading in life."

I grinned. It made sense. I decided to man up and take the next step.

On October 4, 2013, I made my move and invited Barbara on our first date. I picked her up in my Mustang and took her to a café by the harbor. We had a brilliant time, and after that, we started chatting every day, each conversation deepening my feelings for her. I was head over heels in love! She was unique and special. I had never met anyone like her.

Underneath it all, though, I was really afraid of making yet another mistake with a woman, but strangely enough, instead of brooding over it alone, I decided to share my fears and concerns with her. I had inflicted enough pain in the past with poor decisions and wanted to approach this new relationship with transparency.

Barbara listened to me with quiet composure, then said, "Baldur, you'll never find out unless you try. Maybe it's not connecting with me you're afraid of, but your pain from previous relationships."

Seventeen years in a previous marriage had obviously given her a lot of clarity. She must have known something I didn't.

"One thing," I said nervously. "Please don't Google me. Just judge me on the life I'm building now, not my past."

She agreed, but unsurprisingly, my past was not totally avoidable. One Saturday afternoon, I happened to run into her and a group of her friends at the mall. One of them was shocked and didn't hide it-

"Why are you saying hi to this guy? Don't you know he's a murderer? He killed my cousin!"

Iceland is a very small country.

Barbara was stunned. She had never suspected that I'd done time in prison, let alone for an assault with consequences so terrible. Once

she got home, she sat down at her computer. At that very same moment, I had a strange sense that I should call her. It nagged at me. The phone rang for an uncomfortably long time before she eventually answered.

"Hi," I said, not sure of what to say. "What are you doing right now?" "Uh…I'm reading your court documents," she replied tentatively.

I sighed.

I decided to share, there and then, everything about my past. I held nothing back and ended by saying, "Barbara, please know I fully understand if you don't want anything more to do with me."

"Baldur," she replied. "You are not the same man you were. You've made huge changes, and the man you are today is full of love and warmth. I choose him."

I beamed from ear to ear on the other side of the phone. She was just awesome.

That encounter in the mall was just the beginning of the backlash we faced when word got out that we were seeing each other. Adversity came from every direction, but we weathered the storm together as one. One can take on a thousand, but two can take on ten thousand, as it says in the Good Book.

Only ten days after our first date, I asked Barbara, "So...where do I have to apply for permission to marry you?" I just knew we were right for each other. This was totally different from every other relationship I'd experienced. We were a mighty team. We were romantic and supportive and chatted long into the night, reading to each other from the Bible and connecting at the deepest level through our shared faith.

On February 24th, a few months after first setting eyes on Barbara, I started preaching at United Reykjavík. The auditorium was filled with around two hundred people, and I had the stage.

"Today I'm stressed. I'm stressed...and excited...because there's a woman here that I love with my whole heart. A woman who's completely changed my life. Whenever I'm with this woman, I want to become a better man. Barbara, I love you, and I want to spend my life with you!"

I got down onto one knee in front of her, "Barbara, will you marry me?"

She looked me in the eye, smiling knowingly, then nodded her head and accepted. We fell into each other's arms. I stood up and shouted triumphantly into the microphone.

"She said YES!"

Ice and Fire

The auditorium erupted in applause, and my heart nearly exploded. She was mine! We started planning the wedding immediately, settling on July 5th, 2014, as our big day. Barbara had dreamt of a country wedding; we rented out a farm in South Iceland and hosted the ceremony and reception at a nearby hotel.

Our wedding day was one of the most wonderful days of my life. Standing there with pride, I eagerly waited for my bride to walk down the aisle. Then, she appeared – the woman I loved, stunning in her beautiful dress, her 16-year-old son leading the way, her girls carrying baskets of flowers, and my three-year-old stepson holding a sign saying, 'Here comes Mom!' My four-year-old son carried the rings. The guests rose to their feet one after another, singing "Going to the Chapel." It was magic!

My friend, Johnathan, the pastor and former prison guard, married us, and over 200 people showed up to celebrate with us.

We decided to move into my little three-room apartment that I'd been living in with my son…but now we were a family of eight. In the run-up to the wedding, I had told Barbara that I might want to have one more child.

"Baldur," she laughed. "You don't date a 40-year-old woman with six kids and ask for another!" Barbara had long since made her contribution to the world, with five of her own and a foster child who was 3 at the time. Her oldest daughter was 21. When Barbara realized I was serious, though, she eventually relented. "Who am I to deny you a baby when I'm so incredibly good at making them?" We always laughed a lot together, and a sense of humor was always a big part of our relationship. Something that I value to no end.

We decided we'd try for a baby on our wedding night. We set off on our honeymoon after that wonderful day, and together with a great group of friends from the church, we went to a three-week Bible school in Toronto before traveling on our own around the United States, ending up in New York.

In New York, we discovered, to our glee, that our big family was going to be one child richer.

35

OUR LITTLE MIRACLE

During our fantastic trip to Toronto, we met with John Arnott, the founder of the Canadian branch of the 'Catch the Fire' (CTF) churches. I'd been interested in starting up a CTF church in Iceland, and I wanted to get his blessing, so I arrived eager and ready to take notes. John asked me to set aside my notebook and pen. For him, our relationship was the thing that mattered most. This was precisely the kind of church that my wife and I wanted to start back in Iceland - a healthy church family that supported people on their journey toward spiritual, emotional, and relationship health.

After the meeting, John looked at me and smiled, saying, "Baldur, I don't know anybody more suited to open the church in Iceland. With your steadfast wife at your side, I believe this could be a promising beginning to a fantastic, successful project."

Barbara was all in but still slightly concerned. "What does this mean for me? What do I have to do if we take on this church?"

"Just the same as you're doing now," I replied. "Love and help people."

A few weeks after we got home, I realized that it absolutely wasn't that simple. It was a lot of hard work, but we both considered the project exciting and worthwhile, so we kept going.

Then, sorrow came knocking at our door. We lost our unborn baby. The disappointment was very hard on us both, and while the grief did bring us closer together, I had trouble understanding why it had happened.

Maybe God didn't want us to have more children.

Several months later, though, still in pain, God reminded me of a vision I'd had many years before. I had been sitting in prayer on the floor of our church. As I prayed, I saw a little blonde, curly-haired girl in a red raincoat playing. She ran towards me, beaming with joy. I kept seeing flashbacks and images of her. Why was God reminding me of this now, so many years later? Just when I was coming to terms with the fact that I may never have another child.

I told Barbara about it. "I want to try again," I said. "I really want to have a child with you, although I understand if you feel you can't."

And just like that, Barbara was pregnant, and we started on the journey once again. She was afraid and uncertain, though. I could sense it. We had been going to preemptive couple's counseling at the time, which we'd started as soon as I proposed to her. During one of our sessions, the counselor turned to Barbara and asked:

"Could it be that you've always had to live your life closed off and on the defensive? Always ready to defend yourself against pain of any kind?"

Ice and Fire

These words touched my wife deeply. Her background was full of betrayal and rejection, and she realized that her past experiences had caused her to always expect others to hurt or disappoint her.

Later that same day, we were in the kitchen unpacking groceries and talking about the pregnancy when she turned to me and said, "Baldur, just so you know, I'm not going to get attached to this fetus."

I didn't know how to respond.

She fell silent, then explained that she didn't want to get too emotionally invested because it would be too painful if she lost this child too. At the same time, she said she was also determined not to let fear rob her of the joy of expecting a baby. So, after our talk, she put on her jacket and shoes and told me to come with her. We drove into town and went to a children's store. Barbara chose a gown and a little plushy bunny for our unborn baby. I was so proud of her as I watched her actively dismantling the lie that had followed her for her whole life – the lie that everyone would abandon her.

When the time came for our twenty-week ultrasound, everything was just right. Our baby was perfectly healthy.

"Do you want to know the child's sex?" the midwife asked.

We were unsure at the moment, so she sweetly placed a slip of paper in an envelope and gave it to us. I was so curious by the time we got out of the car that I couldn't contain myself.

"Let's check the envelope!"

We tore it open. There was a little note with one word on it.

Girl.

Without me even realizing it, tears ran down my cheeks. "Let's call her Hanna," I said after my beautiful sister. I was absolutely overjoyed. Our unborn baby was healthy, and I was going to get the daughter I'd always dreamed of having.

Neither of us had ever experienced a home birth before, but we decided that was what we wanted for our daughter. All of Barbara's previous pregnancies and births had been smooth and straightforward, so there was nothing to cause us any concern about having Hanna at home.

Then, the big day arrived, and our midwife, Christine, was an absolute godsend. She ran the tub, Barbara went into labor a little under an hour later, and the baby was born within two hours. Barbara was incredible. She delivered Hanna herself. She held her up, and we stared at our precious baby girl's face. We were ecstatic.

Our little miracle had arrived.

36

SOPHIE'S LEGACY

My sister Sophie's path was always one strewn with thorns.

She had really struggled after our sister Hanna's death, and as the years went on, things deteriorated rapidly for her. As well as her drinking issues and a benign tumor she'd had on her brain since childhood, she had sadly become HIV-positive and was also suffering from Hepatitis C. Too much for one person to bear, I felt at a loss as a brother.

One Sunday, she came into the church auditorium unexpectedly. I'd seen her arrive while I was singing and playing music on stage. As soon as I caught sight of her, I noticed the condition she was in. It wasn't good. I was taken aback, and I stopped singing without realizing it, just continuing to play the guitar. As I continued to strum the strings, feeling emotional, I sensed God speaking to me. "Baldur, if she turns around today, I will heal her of all that ails her."

When the service was over, I stepped off the stage, and Sophie walked straight up to me. "Will you pray for me, Baldur?" she asked. Knowing it was all I wanted to do, I replied, "My dear Sophie, are you willing to turn your life around today?"

"Yes," she nodded, looking up at me with exhausted, pained eyes.

Overwhelmed with gratitude, I whispered, "I'm so proud of you, my sister," as I wrapped her in my arms, and we prayed. Right there and then, Sophie faced the challenge of sobriety again. Bravely. Head on. She was broken down, debilitated, and worse for the wear, but I saw only beauty. The beauty that comes from surrender.

From that day on, she started coming to meetings and became an integral part of our church. I loved having her there and saw first-hand how love and simple human kindness can mend the wounds of the heart. Although she was still mostly in a bad way, I knew that with time, God would restore her, and she would find peace and joy again.

At the same time, our brother David was in the middle of a difficult divorce. The mother of his children had started using, and he was left alone, a single father with a considerable history of trauma that had gone completely untreated. As a result, he had started to numb himself too, ending with me and Sophie sitting with him as he lay handcuffed to a hospital bed. He'd been rescued after an overdose and was in critical condition.

We sat with him for hours, our hearts full of fear. The fear of losing another sibling. One afternoon at the hospital, Sophie looked me in the eye and said in a trembling voice:

"I wish I could die instead of him!"

"What? What do you mean?"

"I just don't want my little brother to go through the same agony I did, losing his children and everything he loves so dearly!"

I was left speechless by her comment, but it was so like our Sophie, with her huge, selfless heart, full of love for others.

It was excruciating for me to see our David like that. I felt so powerless. I wished that I could choose for him. Choose life. Choose sobriety. Choose to work through life's suffering. Choose to trust in God. But sometimes, we are just powerless when our loved ones suffer.

David gradually improved, and things went mostly back to normal. I started a new job as a salesman with the country's largest telecommunications company, as well as working for a fintech company with a great salary. We were very happy. Barbara and I bought a new house and planned to move in February 2018, and life seemed to be on the upswing. However, one Sunday afternoon before the move, I was having lunch with my boss when my phone rang.

"Baldur, where are you?"

It was Barbara. I could sense from her tone of voice that something wasn't right. I also saw that I'd missed a call from a friend of ours who worked for an ambulance company.

"What's happened, Love?"

"Can you come straight home?" She said. "Why? What is it?"

"I'll tell you when you get home," she said gravely.

I got in my car. I was certain that someone had died. But who? So many people came to mind. Adrenaline flooded my veins, and my fear intensified. I finally came to a stop outside my house and ran in as fast as I could. Barbara was standing in the middle of the living room with tears in her eyes.

"Darling…it's Sophie," she uttered, her voice breaking. "Greta found her this morning. She was pronounced dead."

Physical agony spread through my body. I couldn't breathe. I stood stiff, motionless, and silent in the middle of our living room. My wife took me into her arms, and I wept in her embrace.

No! No, no, no!

Not again. Not my beloved Sophie. Impossible. No!

Barbara sat me down, and I stared into space as she gathered all of our children into the living room to deliver the tragic news. Overwhelmed, I realized that I would have to notify the entire family that another sister, daughter, cousin, and friend was gone. How could I deliver such devastating news…and for the second time.

David was the first. I watched my brother with tears in my eyes as he came walking into the front hallway.

"What? What's happened?"

"Sophie is dead, David."

"No!" he shouted. "Stop it! Don't say that!"

He let out a piercing cry of agony and fell to the floor. "What are you saying, Baldur?" I bent down, took a seat next to him on the floor and wrapped my arms around him. Together, we wept. Both of our dear sisters were dead, taken from us long before their time.

We knew what we had to do. We had to tell Mom. She occasionally worked as a taxi driver at the time. She had been on a late-night shift and was sleeping when we arrived at her place. She was still groggy when she saw us entering her apartment, but she instantly sensed that something was wrong.

"What's going on, boys?" "Mom…" I broke down.

"Mom…Sophie's dead," I said, my voice soft.

She let out a terrible scream and started pounding on my chest. "No! No! No!"

She kept on crying, her fist blows raining down on me until she had no strength left. Then, she collapsed in heart-wrenching agony. I held her until she was calm. She lay in my arms, utterly shattered.

Daniel, my little brother, stood staring at us. I saw him withdraw even further into himself at the news, tears running down his cheeks. Yet another trauma. As well as recently losing his father, he had been robbed of another sibling. Another source of comfort and refuge…gone. The poor boy was barely 20 years old.

After about half an hour, we helped Mom and Daniel to get themselves ready. We had to go and tell Sophie's boys the terrible news. Soon.

Before anything came to light on social media, on the way there, David called the boys' father, Harold, and asked him to fetch the boys and bring them over immediately because there had been a death – Mom's.

When they arrived, Harold sat down in the living room. The boys followed him in, looking very sad with tears in their eyes.

Harold suddenly stared at my mom, looking confused and, quite honestly, petrified.

"I…I don't understand. Your mom…she's sitting right here. What…what is going on?"

I couldn't work out what he was going on about.

"Yeah, that's Mom," I said. Harold stared at me wide-eyed and confused. "But…I don't…Who's dead then?"

Then, the penny dropped. I felt sick to my stomach. He looked at my face. When we had told him on the phone that 'Mom' had died, he had thought it was my mother - not his boys' mother.

"What?" he groaned. "No. Not Sophie?"

I couldn't bear to look at my nephews. My heart shattered as sorrow engulfed the room, and they all broke down and wept together, confronted by the profound consequences of addiction - the ultimate cost - life itself.

Later, when I went to pick up Sophie's belongings, I thought about the last few days of her life. She had relapsed after arguing with her boyfriend, yet again, and had moved out of his place. She'd sent me a text message saying she'd fallen off the wagon, but I shouldn't worry, as she was now in her room. The people in the rest of the apartment were still on a binge, but she was going to stop there and then sober up and come back to church. That was the last message I ever received from her. She died from withdrawal that very same night. She had vomited and aspirated it into her lungs. The only thing that comforted me was my belief that she was now with her Heavenly Father and in our beloved Hanna's arms.

The strange thing was that three weeks before her death, Sophie had collapsed in her kitchen at home. She called me afterward, obviously frightened and stressed. She thought her brain tumor had maybe started growing and that her loss of consciousness probably had something to do with that. I advised her to get checked out by a doctor. We got the results from her blood tests and brain scan just two weeks before her death. The doctor was confused though, and told her he couldn't fully comprehend them. Her Hepatitis had vanished - she'd been prescribed a course of medication to treat it twice, both times without success - but now it was gone without any medication whatsoever. Her HIV viral load was so low that it was no longer detectable, and the brain tumor…also gone.

I remembered God's words to me as Sophie walked into that church service some months before. The promise that he would heal her of all her ailments if she turned her life around that day. It really puzzled me. Why had God healed her if he knew she would die just a short while later? Then I understood. God had promised to heal all her sicknesses, and he had done just that. The rest was hers.

I reached out to our priest Arnold, who'd buried our Hanna, and told him the devastating news. I said that her funeral had to be full of hope. Just like Sophie was. The hope is that life does not end here. The hope of the Gospel of Jesus. We got a band to play Sophie's favorite songs, and I also played and sang a song that I'd written after losing Hanna.

Arnold spoke about the resurrection of Jesus. How terrible everything seemed on the first Good Friday. Jesus had died on the cross; his disciples scattered, and everyone was let down and believed it was all over. Then Sunday came, and Christ rose from the dead so that we could all be with him in heaven.

Sophie was buried on a Friday, and we all showed up for church that Sunday. Mom, David, Daniel, and I stood in front, holding onto one another. No matter what happened, we stood together and kept praising God.

I wrote a song called 'Live Forever' about a revelation I had that Sunday. A song about how even in the worst moments of suffering, I pull myself close to God and fall at His feet, as he loves away my deepest fear. The fear of losing everyone I love.

As I tried to find some meaning or purpose in Sophie leaving us, I remembered a piece she had written once and shared with me:

This great need for happiness, for peace, has closed us off and made us lonely.

Without stopping, we've walked the path in great hope, in self-deception.

Day after day, in anger, in grief, so often we hear our souls scream out.

So often, we yearn for rest.

We children have dwelt in self-destruction because of our conscience.

This is your fault, says Mom, says Dad.

But we are just the children of alcoholics.

Written by Sophie. 7 August 2005.

As I thought of her words, I was determined not to let death and destruction have the last word in my life.

With Barbara by my side, we embarked on a shared mission - we would work together to extend our hands and listen to lonely souls like Sophie. Counseling them, caring for them, and walking beside them until they found healing in their connection to God.

Broken homes would be restored. Broken families would be reunited. This would become our purpose.

This would become Sophie's legacy.

37

FEARLESS LOVE

When Barbara and I met and fell in love, she'd just completed a three-year university degree and obviously had no idea her life was going to head in the crazy direction it did. She was planning to study addiction counseling in Minnesota and was preparing to apply for a master's degree. Once we started living together as a married couple, she realized that her plan wasn't possible, as it would mean one of us living in the US for a few years, and that wasn't an option for us. She soon found out that the University of Iceland offered a Masters-level program in family therapy. A perfect fit for her, she wasted no time and enrolled.

I was still working in sales, but I really wanted to go in the same direction as Barbara and help people restore their lives. Make some kind of meaningful contribution. I opted to study executive coaching, and at the same time, Barbara and I started our very own counseling company. We called it Hope Counseling.

We worked hard, built the company together, and very quickly started taking bookings for sessions. It was amazing, and I was really pleasantly surprised by the results I was achieving with my clients. Felt like I was finally doing what I was made to do, and it all became very real for me when I was invited to give talks at church conferences in Ireland and England… and would be paid for it. Paid to share my story! The trip was not without incident, though. As we got to the airport, all packed and full of enthusiasm, we discovered that Barbara had brought the wrong passport! There was no way we could make it home to find the right one and make it back on time, but my dear friend Victor offered to take a chance and drive her home. By pure coincidence - or not - a couple of passengers took so long getting out to the plane that Victor and Barbara made it back just in the nick of time! They ran through the airport as fast as their legs could carry them. We boarded the plane, and our heart rates dropped from 120 back down to somewhere near normal. The idea of speaking to an audience in English made me feel a weird mix of nerves and excitement, but the trip went really well and was a huge stride toward realizing my true calling.

From then on, our drive was all about developing our company and offering counselling. We became even more determined after David overdosed and almost lost his life again. I knew that I just had to keep doing the same thing I always did - keep following God, keep praising God, keep fighting the good fight of faith. Sorrow blanketed my family, but day-to-day life had to go on. Barbara and I traveled to Italy to study Emotional Focused Therapy (EFT), a therapeutic method for couples, and we also started a podcast together. We recorded ourselves speaking as a couple, chatting about our own experiences and issues rather than as scholars with heads full of theories. We had a huge amount of fun and learned a lot about each other and ourselves as we openly discussed everything from communication, connection, and codependency to sharing our own funny personal stories.

If there's anything I've learned from my relationships and holding therapy, it's the importance of creating good connections. When we first combined our families, Barbara's girls would stiffen up like popsicles whenever I hugged them. It would have been so easy for me to just pull back, accept their behavior, take it as rejection and just give up. But I didn't … and like tiny drops of water end up making an ocean, we slowly managed to create a wonderful connection between us. I remember as if it were yesterday, one day, one of our boys forgot his swimsuit, so I took it to him at school. When our daughter, a real teenager at the time, saw me in the corridor, she ran into my arms in front of her entire class, hugged me, and told me she loved me. I was gobsmacked! What a beautiful reward for not giving up, for reminding them constantly how lucky I was to have them as part of the package. I was a rich man.

Both our counseling agency and our podcast began to grow and thrive, and Barbara also started working at a family therapy and crisis center. Our vision for both the company and the church was the same - to promote 'family health.' Healthy families create healthy children, who, in turn, build a healthy society. A place where we didn't have to watch on as our young people die long before their time from suicide or addiction-related illnesses. All this led eventually to the creation of an event we called Stay Alive.

It was Barbara who suggested the name Stay Alive. I'd endured far too much pain watching my family fall prey to addiction, and I realized that anger works in two ways. It either causes resentment that turns into bitterness, or it ignites a passion for a worthy cause. We decided to invite the President of Iceland and his cabinet to our event because we wanted to draw attention to the terrible problem so many of our young people were facing. The President came, along with his son, and during his opening address, he spoke about the importance of safeguarding our young people and future generations by focusing more than ever on public health, mental health, and preventative measures. This was so good to hear.

After Stay Alive, the owners of the counseling company that Barbara was working for contacted me to ask about a collaboration. I was still working for the fintech company, and I could have worked my way up the ladder there. But I'd found my niche, and meeting with the owners really got me revved up and excited. I knew my salary would take a hit while we lay down the groundwork, but amazingly, I held 94 counseling sessions during my first month full-time, which meant I'd already made more than I did at my previous job. I was ecstatic! I kept working on my music as well, writing and producing songs.

Serendipity was all around, and everything was falling into place for us.

Barbara and I were happy, working together and bringing God's therapeutic love to others. We eventually started what we call 'Fearless Love' - an international family passionate about seeing people live in their full identity. We believe that everyone was made for greatness, and our vision was to grow a family of fearless warriors all over the world.

Warriors who love themselves and the world around them without fear and shame. Reaching their full potential.

Through our work and the podcast, we really started to see the impact that sharing our personal stories had on couples. The perfect way for people to connect with and understand one another, stories really can stir people's hearts and change people's perspectives in a magical way.

Little did I know that I was on the brink of finding out what a profound impact sharing my story could have on others.

38
DON'T GIVE UP!

In September 2018, an unexpected encounter with a man named Troy Buder marked an incredible turning point in my life. A mutual friend had given him my phone number, and his seemingly casual coffee invitation turned into a most profound exchange and surprising relationship. I didn't really have the time to meet him but felt I should give him at least half an hour on a break from work. There was a pause on the other end of the line before he accepted my offer - he'd booked a trip around Iceland's Golden Circle, a popular scenic tourist route, for the exact time that I'd offered to meet him. He decided to skip the trip and meet me instead, so we planned to meet at a coffee shop in Reykjavik.

As soon as I met Troy, I felt an instant connection with him, an unspoken understanding that I felt beyond our words. After our chat over coffee, we connected so well that I invited him back to my place to finish our conversation. He visited Barbara and me that evening, and gradually, the topic turned to my past, which led to me unraveling the story of my entire life to Troy.

Troy was a film producer, and once I'd finished talking, he looked at me and smiled. "What you don't know, Baldur, is that I focus on making movies with a positive message… and I have to say, I think your story is amazing! It definitely belongs in a book…but I also think there's potential for it to be adapted into a movie."

I was completely stunned.

"Seriously! I mean it!" he grinned. "Start gathering source materials… then sit down and start writing your story."

I stood at the precipice of a new chapter. Filled with purpose, I did what he'd suggested, started collecting documents from hospitals and institutions, and began creating a timeline of my life.

When the lawyer from Child Protective Services called to let me know that my papers were ready, she said -

"I just wanted to let you know; I'm so sorry. It's clear from these files that nobody took care of you, and that's just incredibly sad."

I felt my nasty inner critic begin to terrorize me as I got into the car to fetch the reports - Nobody loved you, remember? You're the black sheep. I ignored it. I went straight home and read all the papers, and the words hit me like a blow to the chest. The interviews and psychologist's remarks about me as a small child were shocking, to say the least. I frequently had to stop reading, put the papers aside and take a long, deep breath.

Nobody seemed to be there for me… she was right. I alternated between rage and tears as I read, but I allowed myself to feel the difficult emotions.

I went through a period of intense anger whenever I pictured that little boy, Baldur, unsupported and broken down, again… and again. The support of my wife was invaluable to me as I went through this heavy process. Until that one morning when I was praying, I heard the familiar quiet voice inside me.

"Do you remember Ed Fernandez?" A smile spread over my face.

"I loved you so much that I sent a man all the way from the Philippines to connect with you and teach you the Lord's Prayer!"

How could I forget? I felt tearful.

That prayer had kept me alive.

That prayer had helped me fall asleep when the anxiety was unbearable. That prayer sparked hope when I started on my journey to sobriety. That prayer had shaped me without my even knowing it.

All along, my heavenly Father had believed in me when nobody else did.

Around that same time, Barbara had been asked to come speak at Symbiosis, a charity that helps with addiction and social difficulties. It was a Thursday evening, and as I looked out across the audience, I soon noticed that Frosti was there. Frosti was the guy I'd once brutalized for not paying up many years before in the park. He'd always refused to meet me, so I'd never had the chance to apologize for the horrific abuse I'd subjected him to. But there he was, standing a few rows behind me.

After her speech, Barbara called me up on stage. I took the microphone and looked in Frosti's direction. Filled with remorse and with tears in my eyes, I asked him for forgiveness in front of everyone. We embraced.

Another wound healed.

A short time later, I got a message from him. He told me that letting go of the anger he'd felt towards me for so long had granted him so much freedom and relief. I was so grateful that I'd been given the opportunity to somehow atone for the pain I'd caused and to let go of that ugly piece of my past.

There are many negative forces in this world that are warring against the human soul. Negativity tries to pull us down into shame, into believing we are unworthy of love, that we are defective, ugly, worthless, or a mistake. But there is a far greater force - Love. God's Love was the amazing antidote to the terrible toxic shame that bound me for so many years. What we must do is never give up! Never surrender to these lies.

It's so terribly sad how many people give up just before their breakthrough, just before the dawn. Just when victory is right around the corner, we need to remember what the Apostle Paul once phrased so well: "In due season, we will reap if we do not give up." Sometimes, you just need to hang in there until the dark night ends.

This book is the story of my dark nights, my defeats, my mistakes. At the same time, though, it's the story of how, God willingly, I never gave up. Luck certainly wasn't always with me…but lucky me, God most definitely was.

"Keep going. Don't give up!"

Looking back, I see the triumphs and disasters that my choices caused, but I also see that I really was doing my best considering my circumstances. I realize too, that everyone who'd been involved in my life and had failed me had also been doing their best with the hand they'd been dealt. My mom is nothing short of a hero, and I am so thankful for my wonderful brothers and family. Living a forgiving life is easier when we embrace this insight.

Here is what I want to leave behind with you…

You've also done your best. It may be a path that's rocky and full of pain in places, but there's a reward, in the end, for those who persevere. My reward has been seeing others embrace their value and realizing that they are worthy of love and belonging.

Ice and Fire

A few years ago, I was invited to Belgium to speak to the inmates in three prisons. To tell my story. I explained how I had lived with the shame that came from all the worthless lies that I had once believed about myself.

Lies that were created in the mind of a desperately unhappy child. I tried to open up the floor to the inmates.

"I don't want you to pray in your seats," I said. "If you don't have the courage to stand now, in front of your fellow inmates, you will lose faith in a few days anyway. I'm asking you to stand boldly and give your whole life to Jesus."

To my surprise, the first person to stand was a famous Belgian rapper.

Then another man stood up. Then another.

And another. And another.

Hardened hearts were melting right in front of my eyes, and tears streamed down my cheeks.

After our incredible journey, this is what Barbara and I live for today. We have the privilege of watching people start believing in themselves. We get to see couples healing and improving their relationships. We get to see dads and moms transform their parenting. We get to see the light in the eyes of desperate people as they finally discover… there is hope.

I have a dream of Iceland being a safe haven. A place of emotional and spiritual security, where strong families reinforce their children's identities and secure relationships are the center of everything. A community built from the inside out. A community where all children are my children, all women are my sisters, and all men are my brothers. A community that nurtures its neighbors - Love your neighbor as yourself. Dismissing people as addicts or alcoholics and pushing them aside is never, ever, a solution.

I remember so well how, in 2016, we all proudly stood by our men's national soccer team during their massive success in the European championships. We were one team - all Icelanders together - and our boys, incredibly, defeated one powerhouse after another. In unity and solidarity, we fought with them from our homes, in front of our screens. I remember laughing at the fact that water usage in the Reykjavík area dropped to next to nothing during the games. We didn't even stop to go to the bathroom because we were all in it together with our soccer boys!

I still have this dream. A dream that goes far beyond individual aspirations. Whatever your unique dream may be, please…keep going. Let hope and determination guide your steps, even in your hardest times. It is possible, and I know that it is with that unwavering spark of crazy perseverance that your dreams can become your reality.

You are not your past. You are not your pain. You are not the violence and abuse you've endured. You are not a perpetrator or a victim. You're so much more than that. These things do not define you.

God is neither far away nor is it complicated to simply talk to Him. Don't give up.

www.ingramcontent.com/pod-product-compliance
Lightning Source LLC
Chambersburg PA
CBHW040305170426
43194CB00022B/2900